Going Nuts
In Brazil with
Jack Douglas

Going Nuts
In Brazil with
Jack Douglas

G. P. Putnams Sons, New York

*This book is dedicated to my dear little wife
Reiko, my two fine sons, Bobby and Timothy—
and Walter Matthau.*

Going Nuts
In Brazil with
Jack Douglas

Special to the New York Times

WASHINGTON, Sept. 14—The United States announced plans today to give Brazil 1.3 million to buy contraceptives. It was the first time this country had ever included funds for that purpose in a foreign aid program.

1

The deck of the riverboat *Lola Falana* was loaded with five hundred cases of U.S. Rubber Company condoms, the weight of which made the riverboat *Lola Falana* hard to maneuver in the tricky currents, side currents, and cross ripples of the Amazon River. A smart fish would have had trouble maneuvering these treacherous waters.

To further complicate navigation the crew of the *Lola Falana*, which had come within a whim's breadth of being called the *Tina Turner,* had been hitting a bottle of Ernest and Julio's best plum brandy that they liberated from a United Fruit warehouse downriver in Belém.

As they had neared the dock where they were to land at the town of Barritos, Brazil, which is about 2,000 miles upriver from the Atlantic, they ran out of brandy and switched to a native drink called Cha made from fermented bananas. It was probably the first bionic beverage. Three drinks and you could leap tall buildings in a single bound. (It's a bird! It's a plane! It's a drunk!)

The first few wildly spectacular landing attempts and the hysterical blowing of the *Lola Falana*'s steam whistle brought people to the town dock from miles around. This was something not to be missed by the entire Barritos population, including me, my little Japanese wife, Reiko, and my two sons, Bobby, fifteen, and Timothy, seven. We all appreciated a well-planned catastrophe.

The captain of the *Lola Falana* was reputed to be a hundred and three years old and was the only Amazon river pilot to wear dark glasses over his contact lenses over his cataracts when he went for his biannual navigational vision checkup, which as a special concession to his longevity, was given to him in braille.

The first pass the *Lola Falana* made at the town dock missed entirely and demolished a canoe full of freshly picked ripe yams and a ripe young girl that the yam picker had future plans for. The yam picker rescued as many ripe yams as he could. When he looked for the ripe young girl she had disappeared—with another yam picker.

The second try was better. The captain managed to swing *Lola's* stern downstream and headed her bow towards the dock, but he was a little closer than he had anticipated and hit the end of the dock dead center—the boat stopped with a sickening suddenness, but the dock kept right on going.

I felt that although it was fun for the children because there wasn't much else to do in Barritos, it was also getting to be a little dangerous, and when the *Lola Falana*'s bowsprit on its third full-stream-ahead try, speared three little Japanese cars which were parked dockside, and Bobby said, "Look, Papa—a Toyota shish kebab!" I thought it was time we were moving on to a safer if less entertaining spot.

Just as we were about to leave this fun scene, there was a wild female scream that seemed to come from the *Lola Falana,* which was now back in the middle of the river and getting ready for another attempt at a navigational triumph—a landing at the Barritos town dock.

"Papa! Look! There's a girl out there!" I thought he meant in the water and I'd have to strip off my clothes and swim madly out there and drown with her. But she was on the boat, and she seemed to have lots of red hair, and I couldn't blame her for screaming—if she was a passenger on the *Lola Falana.*

"I wonder what she's doing out there," Reiko said.

"Screaming," Timothy said. "Come on, let's go home and go swimming."

Our new home is called "Casa Las Bombas" and it's a rubber plantation near the small town of Barritos, Brazil, which is about two-thirds up the Amazon, the world's mightiest and most awesome river.

Reiko and Bobby, Timothy and I live in this old adobe "casa" which used to belong to one of Brazil's richest rubber barons. The grounds are fantastically beautiful, with almost every kind of fruit and flower growing in its five acres of gardens, which surround a magnificent 100-foot swimming pool with a waterfall. The former owner, who went broke, had spared no expense. It was a sort of San Simeon without Marion Davies.

Thousands of crazy unbelievable Brazilian birds keep screaming through the gardens. I don't think they want us there because they know we're strangers, but we're going to stay.

It's quite a change from owning a hotel in Granby Lakes, Maine, which was our unfortunate lot, not too long ago. We wanted to get as far away from Granby Lakes, Maine, as possible, and I think we've succeeded. As the crow flies, Barritos, Brazil, is 6,459 miles from there.

Bobby says that—so far, twenty-three crows have tried, but none of them has made it. Most of them usually give up somewhere around Honansville, Connecticut. They land in Erv Combos' corn field—eat a little of Erv's corn for strength—and then start walking back to Granby Lakes (they take the Appalachian Trail, which is a lot more scenic than the Massachusetts Turnpike and well worth the extra effort to avoid Howard Johnson's).

New England is attractive in the way of a pretty milkmaid, while Brazil is like an exotic houri—sensual, seductive, and explosively flamboyant.

Instead of white birches and red squirrels, Brazil has fan palms, flaming orchids, rubber trees, and the anaconda. The rubber trees are docile enough, but the anaconda is a seventy-five foot boa constrictor, who, if he wishes, can wrap himself around a whole village of pigmitos (small natives) and crush them to bite-size hors d'oeuvres in no time at all. It is a blessing, the Reverend Meech, the local missionary, keeps telling everybody (when he's sober enough), that the anaconda only gets hungry about twice a year. This is the blessing he exhorts them with every Sunday, and this is the kind of blessing that keeps the local natives trusting more in voodoo and witch doctors than The Lord. The Lord, as far as they are concerned, is Hurd Cambridge, an Englishman, who owns four million acres of a Brazilian nut plantation, plus a few Brazilian oil wells, which are giving Venezuela a run for its money in this fuel-freak planet of ours.

Our plantation is comparatively small, and our output of latex (milk) from which, of course, rubber is made, is even smaller, which in a way works out fine because since 1910 there has been no demand whatsoever for Brazilian rubber. The huge plantations in Malaysia and the Dutch East Indies outproduce and undersell Brazilian rubber. Anyone who owns and runs a Brazilian rubber plantation is classified by Dun & Bradstreet under "Hoo-Ha!"—which means exactly what it says.

The main house on our rubber "spread" we have renamed "Casa Las Bombas," which is as close as I can get, in Portuguese, to House of the Big Flop, which doesn't bother us a bit because we've never been happier. All of us, Reiko, Bobby, Timothy, and I, are alive and happy and the people in Barritos don't mind us being here at all—as they did in Granby Lakes, Maine. In Brazil we were accepted immediately, but according to my neighbor in Granby Lakes it takes twenty-eight years for you to be accepted in Granby Lakes (he had two years to go). There's one *other* condition under which they'll accept you up there. If you *die*. As they're lowering you into your grave, they all lean over and spit on your coffin and yell, "We accept you!" This is about as demonstrative as they ever get, which shows that under the harsh down-east exterior they're *all* heart and considerable horseshit.

The five hundred cases of condoms were unloaded from the *Lola Falana* at the Barritos town dock in no time at all (two and a half weeks) by three small boys (ages five, seven, and nine) and the one-hundred-and-three-year-old man (who owns the *Lola Falana* and the town dock and is the father of the three small boys). The mother, I learned, is pregnant with twins, and did not help with the unloading—except during the week. Sundays she spent in the Church of Our Lady of the Amazon and the A&P, praying and lighting candles to the Saint of Infertility. She felt that seventeen children were enough—the rubber business being the way it was.

The five hundred cases of condoms were escorted by an American M.D. Miss Veronica Ramsey, who arrived dressed all in white. She didn't look an M.D. at all. She looked like Miss Universe. Her legs were tan and long. Her skirt was short and her tight white blouse was full of goodies. She had burnished red hair, she was green-eyed, and she moved like a sexy cat. And she didn't talk—she purred. And the male population of Barritos arose to the occasion as one. There wasn't a recumbent penis for miles around. It was like a mass flag-raising at Iwo Jima. This included the three small boys and the one-hundred-and-three-year-old man. It took him all afternoon, but he made it and was rewarded by a round of applause from the docksiders. Foolishly he took a bow and whoosh! the magic moment collapsed like the passing of a giant redwood.

Reiko, when she first saw Dr. Ramsey, said she looked like a Hong Kong hooker.

"What's wrong with that?" I said, as I was by this time being bored by the bare-breasted aborigine-type of buttocky belles of Barritos (and why somebody like Norman Gimbel doesn't write a song "Belles of Barritos" I don't know. He did pretty well with "Umbrellas of Cherbourg" and "The Rumps of Rotterdam").

"I think she's gorgeous," I foolishly continued, and was rewarded by a day of silence and soy sauce on my afternoon yogurt (just before siesta). I spent my siesta lying in a bathtub of warm water and four pounds of Alka-Seltzer (try it some time—it's better than a whirlpool bath except that one tends to keep turning bottom side up from the bubbles).

No one knew what was in those interesting five hundred cases stacked on the dock. The words "Have fun!" had been graffitied on each box by some fancy-free U.S. longshoreman in New Jersey, but the words were scribbled in English, and English is a language which is as completely baffling to the Portuguese-speaking Brazilians, as Portuguese is to English-speaking Americans. "Portuguese," to quote Lord Byron, "is a language to be used only when house-breaking an iguana."

Hurd Cambridge, by way of welcoming the apparently lubricous Dr. Veronica Ramsey to Barritos-on-the-Amazon threw a lavish bash, which started on Friday and ended on Monday, some people remembered later. Much later.

The Cambridge hacienda was miles from its front gate, and as Reiko and I drove to it, along a beautifully paved blacktop driveway, the trees on both sides of the road seemed to get closer and closer.

"Those are nut trees," I explained to Reiko, hoping I was right. They were getting so thick and close I started to imagine they were giant meat-eating plants that hadn't had a good meal in years and were reaching out with their voracious tendrils towards our little open-top Volkswagen.

"They're drooling," Reiko said in a very small voice. I thought they were, too, but I said, "It's damp—that's dew."

"Look out!" Reiko was screaming now, "a snake!"

I slammed on the brakes so hard my air bag blew my head back against my headrest and broke my neck and Reiko, who doesn't believe in air bags, went flying over the windshield, and had her trip halted in midflight by a perfect collision with a giant anaconda. The anaconda, who had been peacefully dozing while dangling almost his full length from a nut tree, got the hell out of there quick. He had just eaten a whole wild pig and was in no mood for dessert—like a little Japanese girl who had come from nowhere *smack* into his *wild pig!*

Reiko screamed for a while, and after I convinced her that anacondas are an endangered species and do a lot of good in the jungle, she calmed down to a few whimpers. I tightened my turtleneck sweater to keep my head from rolling away, and we drove the last two miles to Hurd Cambridge's regal hacienda.

The driveway in front of the Cambridge place was jammed three deep with some of the fanciest, and weirdest collection of cars I had ever seen. From a 21st Century Silver Cloud Rolls to a 1908 Electric—powered by a single dry cell and steered by an oar.

We parked our battered little Volkswagen next to a shiny 1938 Studebaker with monkey-fur seat covers, driven by a creature, who with very little effort could have been a Neanderthal, and who carried a loaded and cocked .45 automatic on his right hip. His left hip was unadorned except for a naked, razor-sharp, three-foot machete.

"Expecting trouble?" I asked him. He just laughed, and his eyes lit up with hopeful anticipation.

2

Hurd Cambridge, who reminded me very much of Richard Burton before Richard switched to waitresses and other assortments, greeted us with genuine warmth, which we had no way of knowing he really felt—deep down. He embraced me Mafia style, kissed Reiko on both cheeks, and pointed us in the direction of a mile-long bar.

The bar was jammed with rather sweaty people. (This part of the Amazon valley had not become famous for any kind of air conditioning—although there was something hanging from the ceiling that looked like a propeller from the Queen Mary, which turned slowly clockwise and disturbed the atmosphere not one bit.)

Reiko and I had lived among these people for almost a year and we knew many of them. Hurd Cambridge's wife, Elizabeth, a lovely English-complexioned beauty, was shrieking with mirth at the far end of the long bar, apparently convulsed by something said by the Reverend Meech, who—as Barritos gossip repeated again and again, had sustained a hard-on for Hurd's wife ever since he arrived there some ten years before, with his wife, Norma-Lee. Norma-Lee, nowhere to be seen, was a one-time Southern belle and was either very naive or very tolerant of the Reverend Meech's never ending pawing of Elizabeth Cambridge's magnificent rump, and running patter of bald innuendos of his steamy desire.

Elizabeth Cambridge did not welcome the Reverend Meech's crudities, not did she discourage them. She, I'm sure—again from local gossip—was considered the local nympho. Anything male and available was welcome. Anything except the Reverend Meech. For some reason he never made the honors list.

"Good evening, good people." It was his honor, Señor Casseres, the mayor of Barritos.

"Good evening, Mr. Mayor," Reiko and I said, respectfully. Señor Casseres was a smallish man who looked like a Portuguese-Spanish-Indian Adolphe Menjou, and he dressed the way that Menjou did—back in 1928—wide shoulders and pointed shoes. He even had Menjou's little waxed mustache, although on Mayor Casseres, it was more Chaplin than Menjou.

"Any news from the capital?" I asked the mayor.

"Very little, very little," the mayor admitted sadly. And everybody but the mayor knew why he almost never heard anything from Brazil's magnificent capital city, Brasília. Firstly—Brasília may be the capital of Brazil, but it was built by some dreamers *way back* in the Brazilian bush, and nobody wants to live there. They want to live in Rio—where the action is. Also, every time Mayor Casseres sends messages to Brasília, and he sends them by the hundreds, to be hand-delivered by messenger—the messenger, who has never had any intention of making the two-thousand-mile round trip to the capital city just to deliver a message from the mayor of Barritos, simply runs down a jungle trail until he is out of the mayor's sight and then he tosses his dispatch case into the river and goes back to his little grass shack and makes love to whomever is available. And there is plenty available because they are very impressed by his red, gold-braided, messenger's uniform which jangles loudly with many decorations for meritorious and faithful, speedy service.

The mayor introduced us to the Barritos chief of police, an individual who looks and acts like Pancho Villa at his peak. Chief of Police, Señor Bocachica, is a walking arsenal. How he can walk at all is a mystery. He carries six pistols in various holsters made specially to suit each physiological locale. Most notable is his crotch gun, the holster of which was designed specially to safeguard against the weapon being accidently pointed in the wrong direction in the event that the chief fell downstairs in pursuit of some chicken thief or somebody's wife. A bullet in the wrong spot at the wrong time could spoil EVERYTHING.

"How's crime?" I asked Señor Bocachica, not expecting a too exciting report.

"Very nice," Señor Bocachica answered, "very nice." Señor Bocachica had just spoken the only English he had ever learned, so if the night before some Brazilian nutpicker had gone berserk and murdered his whole family, plus every other family on his street, Señor Bocachica would report it as "very nice." Actually, when you think about it, it's a helluva lot more pleasant than hearing the real story every night on the six o'clock news.

"What are you drinking, Jack?" asked Mr. Brown, who was another plantation owner, and at the moment seemed to be acting as bartender.

"A little brandy," I said, "and what are you doing behind the bar?"

"It's my hobby," Mr. Brown said in his thick German accent, which seemed to sprout more Teutonisms every time I saw him. I'm sure that "Mr. Brown" had been "Herr Braun" back in the Black Forest or wherever he came from in Germany. Nobody could ever get him to talk about his past.

"Maybe there's a reason," Reiko said.

"Like what?"

"Like he's a German spy."

"Who came in from the cold?" I said.

"What?"

"It's just a joke. There was a book called *They Spy Who Came In From the Cold* and I said—because it's so goddamn hot down here and—"

"Never mind," Reiko said, and I'm glad she did.

"Brandy," Mr. Brown said, "how about you, Madame Douglas?"

"Liquor always make me sick. I'll have a scotch and soda," Reiko said.

While Mr. Brown was pouring Reiko's drink which I knew she would not drink, I don't know why I did it but I did—I raised my glass and said to Mr. Brown, *"Heil Hitler."*

Mr. Brown didn't turn a hair. He just handed Reiko her drink and said, *"Niemand wohnt hier unter diesem Namen."*

Reiko said, *"Jawohl!"* downed the scotch in one gulp. And was sick.

Hurd Cambridge did not pinch pennies when it came to throwing a party. Champagne flowed like the Amazon. Waiters were everywhere, and a seventy-three piece marimba band played without halt, costing Hurd at least a hundred thousand cruzeiros, or about fourteen dollars and thirty-two cents. The musicians were nonunion and nonbright. And I felt, as the night progressed, that a seventy-three piece marimba band was about seventy-two too many. Especially as they only knew one tune that they could all play together. Eighteen and a half hours of La Cucaracha was more than enough. Not that anyone cared what the band was playing—the dancing was anything from a Strauss-type waltzing to a modernized (1923) Lindy Hop, with a little limbo thrown in on the side, which did nothing for the tidiness of the ballroom floor. Most limboers crashed on their first try and had to be stacked in one corner until they regained consciousness. If some of you don't know what limbo dancing is, see page 23 of the new *Columbia Dictionary.* They don't know either.

"So glad you could come." It was Elizabeth Cambridge, Hurd's never-faithful wife. "It wouldn't be a party without you and Reiko," Elizabeth Cambridge crooned in her throaty orgasm-toned voice, never looking in Reiko's direction. As she spoke, she slowly rotated her hips massaging herself into a state of everready throb.

"So nice of you to ask us," I said, trying to bow with my old world charm, which I had copied from an old English movie where Sir Walter Raleigh was being presented to the Queen for the first time. (The *last* time he bowed to the Queen somebody let him have it in the back of the neck with a chain saw.)

"You remember Cousin Shapiro," Elizabeth Cambridge said, as she undulated into another group of merry-makers and left us with a little half-Jewish-half-Chinese man who was the proprietor of Barritos' only army and navy store. We didn't know it at the time, but Cousin Shapiro had many sidelines, one of which was working for the Israelis—tracking down war criminals in South America. He was also employed by the People's Republic of China, and supposedly sending them secret information, setting things up for the big takeover, which would happen whenever the People's Republic was ready.

"How are you tonight?" Reiko asked Cousin Shapiro. "I'm Reiko Douglas—I'm Japanese."

"Ah, so," Cousin Shapiro said.

"I'm supposed to say that," Reiko said.

"I know," Cousin Shapiro said, "but what difference does it make—all Orientals look alike."

"What about Mao Tse-tung and Miyoshi Umeki?" I said.

"Exactly," Cousin Shapiro said. "May I bring you some punch or would you care to dance or buy a lottery ticket or maybe put in an order for a Toyota?"

Cousin Shapiro was nothing if not enterprising. He never let a party interfere with business.

"I saw you talking to Mr. Brown," Cousin Shapiro said, trying to appear casual though he only succeeded in looking Chinese and Jewish.

"Yes," I said. "Seems to be a nice chap."

"Did you—" Cousin Shapiro lowered his voice and stood very close to my chest (like I had a microphone pinned to my underwear). "Did you find out anything?"

"Yes," Reiko said. "You can't grow coffee around here."

"He didn't say that," I said.

"I know," Reiko said, "but he's always out there—somewhere in the forest trying experiments—growing something."

"Ah, so," Cousin Shapiro said, wisely, tapping his nose with his forefinger. He tapped it so long I thought he was sending someone a message in Morse code.

"Why do you always say 'Ah So' if you're Chinese?" Reiko wanted to know.

Cousin Shapiro tapped a sign-off on his nose, fanned himself thoroughly with an Oriental fan, then bowed out of sight.

"You know what I think," I said. "I think there's more to Cousin Shapiro than meets the eye."

"Yes," Reiko said. "That fan he was using was made in *New Jersey*."

I didn't know how to answer this so I took the coward's way out and ordered another brandy. Double.

3

Dr. Veronica Ramsey and her fantastic boom-boom bosoms were of course the guests of honor at the Cambridge party. Every one in Barritos wanted to welcome her, except the women in Barritos. They felt that Dr. Ramsey was pure silicone with chrome tips (that's the way they looked under her navel-cut sequinned evening gown). They swung high, low, and wild with every move of her feline body, but somehow they never popped into full public view, as the entire population of male viewers at Cambridge's "Welcome Dr. Ramsey to Barritos" party hoped and prayed they would. Some of the men even ran outside to the life-sized statue of Saint Maria las Grande Tetons de las Andes and lit a few candles of supplication.

Dr. Ramsey further tantalized the party by refusing to reveal the contents of the five hundred cases of whatever (so far as Barritos knew) that were stacked on the town dock.

"In due time," she purred, "in due time. And you're all going to be very pleased." She made it sound like a shipment from Fredricks of Hollywood, who had thought of a new spot to slit open in his fall line of slanty panty-hose, naughty-nighties and booby-boosters. The men of Barritos purred along with her. They could hardly wait. And that included me. I love Reiko, but I'm no different than any other man. I'm an alleycat.

"Christ all Jesus," said Pierre Leuthold, a young Swiss medical student, who was in Barritos to gather material for a paper on the sex habits of the South American Indian, and who had all the statistical curiosity of Kinsey, along with the porno philosophy of Dr. Reuben and Masters and Olsen and Johnson, and had high hopes of suddenly developing into a Harold Robbins-Irving Wallace or better so he could write the sexiest novel of all time and get the hell out of medical school and live a little.

"Christ all Jesus," Pierre Leuthold said again, then, "all she needs is a good fuck!"

"Speak for yourself, Pierre," I said.

"I am! I am!" Pierre said, and headed for the nearest Cambridge bathroom—jogging most of the way.

"What happened?" Reiko said.

"Pierre has finally found a good reason to go on living." I said.

"What's that mean?"

"What's anything mean?"

"What's that mean?"

"It means a little brandy never hurt anybody, and I think it should be legalized."

"Jack," Reiko said, "are you getting drunk?" Reiko had given me an idea.

One week later at the Barritos Opera House, which used to be the opera house where Caruso, Galli-Curci and Madame Schumann-Heink belted out *Carmen, Pagliacci* and *Tannhäuser* way back when Barritos had been the rubber capital of the world, Dr. Veronica Ramsey told her story to an audience, of thousands it seemed. From the whitest of caucasians to the blackest of the aborigines and Indians.

"Ladies and Gentlemen," Dr. Ramsey said, after the tumult of her entrance during which her no bra-ed bosoms had bounced from the wings to center stage. They bounced to a pronounced rhythm, accompanied by bongo drums, jungle percussion, and the beating of hollowed-out logs carried by more than two thirds of this Amazonian audience. No one, I learned later, had planned this rhythmic accompaniment—it just seemed to these simple savages the thing to do. Never had Blaze Starr or Tempest Storm's wildest mammary flinging been accompanied by such definite and precise punctuation.

"Ladies and Gentlemen," Dr. Ramsey had to repeat, "I'm sure you are all wondering why you are here tonight."

This precipitated another demonstration. Like one Elton John never got. Anywhere else it would have been considered the start of a revolution, but here in Barritos where emotions are not leashed, it was simply a tribute to the perfect pair.

"Down on the town dock," Dr. Ramsey continued, "are five hundred cases of condoms—contraceptives—sent here through the courtesy of the United States government, and with love from the United States Rubber Company of Akron, Ohio."

This announcement was followed by silence, then suddenly the audience as a whole was whispering to each other. "What the hell????" seemed to be the main theme. They hadn't the slightest idea of what a condom was or what contraceptives are. They didn't know whether the United States was being good to them or trying to lower the price of Brazilian coffee.

Dr. Ramsey understood that she was not getting through and asked Hurd Cambridge to come out on the stage and interpret. Which he did. There still was no visible sign of understanding. Dr. Ramsey through Hurd asked for a volunteer from the audience. The volunteer quickly emerged.

"No. No," Dr. Ramsey said, "no children!" Hurd Cambridge quickly advised Dr. Ramsey this was not a child but a full grown Pygmy man. This did not sit well with Dr. Ramsey, but there were no other volunteers, and the audience was cheering "Mogo! Mogo! Mogo!" who was the Chief of the Pygmies and the father by seven wives of thirty-nine children.

"Oh, dear!" Dr. Ramsey said, "What luck!" She quickly removed a Ramses number three from its little purple box, and gave it to Mogo—chief of the Pygmies, who promptly slipped it over his tiny head, at the same time screaming with delight "Shower cap! Shower cap!" and disappeared through a handy side door, presumably headed for the nearest YMCA.

Dr. Ramsey didn't call for any more volunteers that night, but she tried to explain the dangers of overpopulation. Using India as an example, she flashed a photo of Mahatma Gandhi on a movie screen and everybody laughed at the old man wearing diapers. Then she flashed another shot of thousands of emaciated Hindus bathing in the Ganges. The new silent audience seemed very disappointed that no great white shark appeared to stir up a little action.

Ever since *Jaws* this seems to be a worldwide phenomenon—anywhere there is water, people have come to expect the great white shark. It's made everyone apprehensive. Most of my friends in Beverly Hills, I've heard, have given up their swimming pools—or filled them with Jello and are inviting people over for Strawberry skinny-dips (bring your own whipped cream).

I heard something else about the movie crowd—Barbra Streisand has *her* pool filled with seltzer and barracuda. —Anything goes wrong at the studio, she invites the whole group over for brunch and a swim. They swim *first*. —Saves a lot on lunch.

Dr. Ramsey's lecture was not a success from her point of view, but for the male population of Barritos it was a night to remember, especially after, at the suggestion of Hurd Cambridge, when she summoned the native witch doctor, Dr. Momomoomoo, to the stage. Momomoomoo wasn't his name, but that was as close as the English-speaking get to his unpronounceable AMA name.

Momomoomoo the witch doctor was a wise old man. He understood not one word of what Dr. Ramsey was explaining as she showed him a condom, but he knew it was something to do with sex, and he kept trying to mount Dr. Ramsey, which was very difficult because Dr. Ramsey would not cooperate, and also because Hurd Cambridge kept beating him over the head with his riding crop, which stimulated the good witch doctor immensely.

Dr. Ramsey was a good sport about the whole thing, but she called for a blackout in the auditorium and during this thirty-second interval, Momomoomoo disappeared for the rest of that night.

4

Some of my readers are very curious (odd may be a better word) and will, after finishing this book, send me a lot of unreadable (some of it unprintable) mail asking me—why, after living in California, Connecticut, Canada, and Maine, which have *something* in common, we suddenly pick up and travel thousands of expensive miles to the vast interior of a remote area of South America. The only answer to this is "why not?"

One of the reasons we moved to this former opulent city on the upper Amazon is to, as I think I said before, get as far away from the scene of our recent unpleasant life in Granby Lakes, Maine, and also, if judgement day is as close as Oral Roberts and Jimmy Carter's sister say it is, we feel that Granby Lakes is going to get it *first* and we want to be as far away from there as possible.

Also, we would like to find out, through personal experience, whether there *is* a perfect place in the world in which to live, which is probably futile, like the young girl slowly but surely turning into an old maid through that other exercise in futility, waiting for "Mr. Right" to come along. Just waiting can bring on a lot of surprises—like what happened to Grace Ziegler, a fanatic super-virgin in Santa Rosa, California, who, for years, it seemed, had been saving herself for "Mr. Right" and suddenly—one Saturday night—found herself being gang-banged by the Santa Rosa Motorcycle and Social Club for the *eighth* time, and had come to realize during the ninth, tenth and eleventh time that screaming about it won't help. You just have to bend over and enjoy it. That's what we are attempting. After our fantastic screwing in Maine, we resolved never to resist again. Now we would just bend over and enjoy it.

27

Maybe.

This is an admirable philosophy, but only if you're feeble-minded. It just doesn't work. Not for me, anyway. Here in Barritos, from the time I arise in the morning until that glorious moment when I slip into my new water bed (whose gentle lapping sound keeps me awake all night), I am *not* bending over and enjoying it. Actually I am on the verge of a complete mental breakdown, brought on by the simple everyday exigencies of life (which, it seems—no matter where you run to—you cannot escape).

I try not to show the turmoil within. I am cool, collected and poised, and try to remember that "poise is *grace* under *pressure*," which brings us right back to Grace Ziegler, the girl who was gang-banged in Santa Rosa. Grace Ziegler, according to the boys of Santa Rosa, had protected her virginity ever since she was five years old as if it were some precious heirloom, like a jar of home-preserved petrified cling-peaches handed down from generation to generation from her great-great grandmother. Grace, like that jar of peaches, couldn't be opened by anything human until that fateful Saturday night when she wiggled her beguiling little ass once too often as she passed Santa Rosa's Elm Street Pool Hall.

That did it!

The next scene in the fascinating drama was played in the Santa Rosa rock quarry—with a cast of thousands—so it seemed to Grace Ziegler. At first she screamed for help. This was just before she screamed for more.

After this traumatic experience, Grace Ziegler decided to have it both ways—she bought a Honda Fireball, which could go 187 miles per hour anytime she wanted it to, and she also became a nun. The best of two worlds, she figured.

But even before our return from Maine, where our electric meter was read by a guy with a seeing eye dog, where the Granby Lakes Town Tax Board decided that we could handle the town's fiscal budget all by ourselves and where ten cords of firewood disappeared from our wood yard just before winter set in, we started to revise our philosophy of bending over and enjoying it, which may have been the principal reason for our complete change of locale and environment and the old "the grass is greener on the other side" viewpoint, which is another crock. Grass is the same color everywhere. Brown.

The novelty of living in the exotic atmosphere of Barritos and in the vast jungle state of Amazonas, in northwestern Brazil, soon became commonplace in our ordinary, everyday lives. We were living exactly as we had lived back in Honansville, Connecticut. Up in the morning with Reiko, Bobby, and I snarling unpleasantly. Timothy was the only one to greet the new day with whoops of joy. He lived for the moment and every moment of the day was the best.

By moving from the rolling miniature hills of the Berkshires to the vast emptiness of the Amazon back country, we had changed nothing but locale. But we did have a lot more space and larger mosquitoes. In Brazil, the mosquitoes attack 747s. Successfully.

Also our "big move" had changed our financial picture and not for the better. Although we were living like feudal barons in the midst of our thousands of acres in a house that rivaled J. Paul Getty's in area if not in style—he had had moats and turrets and drawbridges and courtyards, while we had adobe, and tile and patios.

I had heard of the government's $1,500-a-year personal-pension plan a little too late and had managed to make only one payment. And the few foreign royalties from my books and my music from countries like Uganda, Upper Volta, Lower Slobbovia and Tierra del Fuego, came in such exotic currency that merely depositing it in a bank became a major headache. My friend at Chase Manhattan slowly changed to a mere acquaintance. How we managed to pay our household staff (of five) and our many rubber workers was a miracle in itself, but somehow with sweet talk and promises we made it.

I am exaggerating somewhat, but our finances were very much in jeopardy because of the extreme unpopularity of Brazilian rubber, which I blame entirely on its inaccessibility. From where we tapped our trees, it was a good ten miles to the boat dock in Barritos and then another two thousand or more miles down the Amazon to the sea port of Belém, which itself was up river sixty-eight miles from the open sea, and another five thousand or so miles to Akron, all of which, even with a U-haul trick, would tend to put the price of the unprocessed Brazil rubber up, substantially.

If we hadn't raised our own vegetables, and hogs, sheep, and cattle, we would have been in trouble. As it was, we were in big trouble anyway, concerning the hogs, sheep and cattle. They came to be such pets that there could be no slaughtering. Just a lot of hay, corn, alfalfa, garbage and slop for the hogs—plus plenty of petting and loving. And scratching of ears.

Vegetables have always been the mainstay of the Japanese diet, and Reiko had so many enticing and delicious ways of preparing them, the animals had nothing to fear from us cannibals. But I'll have to admit that rice pudding three times a day could make for satiety, especially if the rice pudding came after a three-course dinner of rice soup, rice patties, and rice burgers—served on rice buns.

The diet was monotonous, but our everyday living was not. Just keeping track of *who* was the government that day could keep you hopping. It could also keep you wary. Would they be friendly, or would search and seizure suddenly become the popular sport of the Brazilian military? Nothing ever seemed to happen along these lines in Barritos. I don't think they cared. Or else the wireless to Brasília—the nutty capital city they had rashly built halfway between Rio and Mato Grosso, which was halfway between Nowhere and Oz—had broken down. Brasília had a population of two. One was the janitor. The other one wanted to know which way to the beach?

I think Brazil was the first place we have lived that Reiko really liked the people. Always in other locales where we have lived either by choice or because they were convenient to whatever I was working on, Reiko developed dislikes for certain citizens. In New York City of course, we had many friends, mainly from television (when television was in New York instead of from a California orange grove).

After being burglarized and robbed of the Russian Crown jewels, which I had been guarding since 1918, we decided to move to the lovely suburban (and rich) village of New Canaan, Connecticut, where we were burglarized again—the first week we were there. They got the Hope Diamond this time, plus the Empress of India, and a wristwatch which had been given me gratefully by Grace Kelly for a superb sexual performance during the making of a porno movie that we had done together before we had gone on to becoming royalty—each in his own way.

After this we moved once again, above Danbury—the real Connecticut frontier.

We spent a couple of years in Honansville, a beautiful little village among rolling hills and fat asses, or to put it another way—the fat hills and rolling asses. They seemed interchangeable after awhile and after awhile I had had enough.

The northern Canadian bush country was our next move. Our nearest neighbor was sixty miles away and in a wheelchair—this suited Reiko perfectly—there would be no friendly neighbor dropping around for coffee. Or so it seemed until anybody and everybody who owned a bush plane found out where we were. Then it was murder. We'd have five and six Cessna 180s tied up to one of our three docks. We lived on a secret lake known only to God and anybody who could fly a plane—which included the guy in the wheelchair. He took the top off our chimney a couple of times, but he landed all right, and his favorite saying, which he repeated over and over was, "Any landing you can wheelchair away from is a good landing." I could have murdered him (and I did)—pushing him and his wheelchair right off the end of the dock into deep water. Nobody missed him except the Royal Northwest Mounted Police—they keep asking the wheelchair company questions about faulty brakes and all that.

Granby Lakes, Maine, the Disneyland of the North, was next on our search for the perfect place to live. And Granby Lakes, Maine, let me say, *is* the perfect place to live if you're a moose, because in Granby Lakes, Maine, moose are protected. But nobody else is. Granby Lakes, Maine, has some real advantages if you have any legal difficulties. Witnesses are cheap (they have no union), but taxes—if you weren't born in Granby Lakes, Maine—will make you wish you had been. Outsiders are taxed by the day, the week, the month, the year, and by the pound. And if you complain about your taxes, they immediately arrange a hearing—at the nearest institution for the deaf.

We left Granby Lakes, Maine, after we could no longer endure the hooliganism of the adjoining golf course owner. We never did find out what his problem was (besides himself), but I felt that after our children, Bobby and Timothy, and our neighbor's children had been threatened by this unpredictable, apparent psychotic, or by his equally kinked partner, and his employees, it was obviously time to leave. Up to our necks in the legal difficulties engineered by four gentlemen from the legal profession (names? just write to me), we took the easy way out and left everything—including our life savings.

Which calls to mind what Melvin Belli, the famous San Francisco lawyer said, after being vindicated of a false accusation. "What are you going to do now?" a reporter asked, and Mr. Belli replied, "I'm going after the guys who did this to me." Mr. Belli believes that revenge is sweet. And he may be right—one of these days, I think maybe I'll call Mr. Belli and find out how much revenge I can afford.

5

Casa Las Bombas, our rubber plantation, is just ten miles from Barritos, and covers some thirty-two thousand acres, which we bought for $1.50 per acre (not being a veteran I had to put 15¢ down) from a man whom IBM was transferring. He had to make a quick sale, and we were glad to take advantage of this. We answered his ad in *Rolling Stone,* and despite the mild screaming, and weeping and wailing of Reiko, who knew by instinct that I was making the mistake of a lifetime (again). She's a born Monday-morning quarterback. A hundred and fifty-six Mondays later.

"What do we know about rubber?" was one of her very good arguments.

"What's there to *know*?" I shot back at her—covering my ignorance with bravado, a method for which I have found excellent use during all my years as a papier-mâché pundit.

After this I quickly retired to my library and volume 19 of the *Encyclopaedia Britannica* (Rayn to Sarr) to study rubber.

I studied rubber a helluva lot more after we had spent the first six months in the state of Amazonas. I found there was a helluva lot more to harvesting rubber than just letting it drip out of a tree into a bucket and airmailing it to Akron. Maple syrup comes like that (after a little boiling in Vermont) but a rubber tree is different from a maple tree. In the first place, rubber was discovered by Columbus, but Maple syrup was discovered by Aunt Jemima. She *had* to—a stack of wheats would taste like round thermal underwear if you didn't disguise them with something sticky and sweet.

Columbus, on his second visit to South America, was amazed to see the native Indians playing tennis with a black heavy ball made from a vegetable gum. He reported months later to Queen Isabella that these black heavy balls rebounded so briskly that they appeared to be alive.

"I'd like to see one of those balls," the story goes.

"I'm sorry, ma'am," Columbus reportedly said, "but we don't have any left."

"What the hell does that mean?!" Isabella screamed, "What happened to them?"

"When, Queen," Columbus said, "—it was a long trip home and—well—we found out that playing tennis on the poop deck of the *Santa Maria* just didn't work out—no backstops." And that, according to historians, is why Columbus found himself chained to a net post of the huge brand-new un-used (red-surfaced) Royal tennis court (in old Barcelona).

So much for the *history* of rubber. The practical side of raising rubber is a little more complicated, although not as complicated as the date palm (as in Indio, California), where nothing happens unless you plant a female date palm next to a male date palm. Some wise-ass just said, "I know, the male is the one with the nuts." Wrong. They both have nuts—that's why it's so complicated—you need a date palm sexer—who costs one hundred and fifty dollars an hour to sort your males and females out for planting. So forget dentistry for your kids—send them to where they'll really make the big buck—date palm sexing school.

With rubber trees (ninety trees to the acre) sex has nothing to do with their output. Rubber trees should yield four to five pounds of rubber each year. If a rubber tree doesn't meet this quota you just give them the old Stalin one-two, "Produce or *die!*" I don't like to think about the number of rubber trees I had to have killed (by a painless method), but as a rubber planter I was forced to be realistic. And ruthless.

The climate around Barritos was excellent for rubber, with growing temperatures between 70 and 90 degrees and about 100 inches of rain a year. This is a lot of rain and tends to make things very green. Moss grows everywhere (if you don't use Arrid. And steel wool).

The rubber trees thrive on the wet, except when all the leaves suddenly fall off. This is a disease particularly associated with the rubber tree and it's called "leaf fall." Botanists and others have been working for many years to find a cure for leaf fall, but there seems to be nothing the rubber planter can do except Elmer's glue the leaves back on and drink vodka—straight. This doesn't solve anything, but the days just fly by.

If the reader doubts the veracity of this fascinating anecdote, let him stop any rubber planter on the street in the Times Square area and ask, "Do you think the rain causes leaf fall or do you think leaf fall causes the rain?" You'll probably get some interesting answers, and also mugged.

Our evenings at Las Bombas plantation were spent sometimes watching television (there was a station at Manaus which wasn't too far downriver from Barritos). The shows were mostly from the United States dubbed into Portuguese, which added a new dimension to *Hogan's Heroes* and the talk shows. Merv, Mike, and Johnny all sound alike because the dubbing was apparently done by the same voice. Sometimes things got a little screwed up and Walter Cronkite became Yma Sumac.

Most of our evenings, especially when it was raining, we were visited by our neighbors, one of whom turned out to be the local bandit, who called himself El Jaguar (after the car—not the animal). El Jaguar, or "Pete" as we called him, posed as labor organizer in the style of California's Cesar Chavez of "Don't buy grapes" fame.

Pete El Jaguar latched onto Reiko and me and Bobby and Timothy because, he said, he could trust us. Trust us in *what* he never said, but he told us many wild tales of highjacking riverboats and sticking up the Barritos-Amazonas State Bank (he hid his identity by wearing a ski mask and painting his toenails). Pete usually brought along a little group of what looked like apprentice banditti—all carrying pistols and dull machetes, and wearing their mustaches long. He also brought the prettiest girls in all of Amazonas. Most of them were stunning mixtures of Portuguese, Italian, Spanish, Dutch, and Indian.

Their undulated entrances were accompanied by an aura of goat's milk that seemed to fill the room, but their sensual femaleness and their grace of movement transformed the aroma of goat's milk to the

Balm of Gilead, the balsam of Mecca, and the "perfumed tincture of the roses," which is a roundabout way of saying "it didn't matter how they smelled 'cause they tasted delicious." (According to Pete El Jaguar.)

The Reverend Meech, a missionary sent to Barritos many years before, to convert the heathens to Christianity or whatever, had long since forgotten about all that and converted himself into an enjoyer of the pleasures of Barritos—whatever turned up. He did make the pretense of a Sunday service that lasted all of half an hour and consisted mainly of the Reverend's relentless reminders to his sparse congregation that they'd all go to hell, and he'd see to it personally, if they didn't come across with a few more cruzeiros for the collection plate. The Sunday service wound up with the singing of that grand old hymn "Bringing in the Sheaves" sung in half Portuguese and half Mato Grosso. The final effect was like the sound of someone beating a cat to death with another cat. It was rhythmic, but it sure wasn't musical.

The Reverend Meech spent hours at our casa after we had first met him at a party given by the ever-ready party-giver, Hurd Cambridge, to welcome Reiko and me and our kids to the region. The Reverend Meech, after an hour or so at the Cambridge bar, introduced himself to us. "I'm the Reverend Henry Meech, of the Church of the Holy Phallus," he said.

"What????" I said.

6

"Everybody always says WHAT?????" the Reverend Meech continued, "but I'll explain—" he was saying this between long gulps from what looked like a quadruple martini (with a drunken goldfish in it). "When I got my diploma from the Downtown Divinity School in Tijuana, it entitled me to choose any religion I wished. I chose the Order of the Holy Phallus."

"I don't understand," Reiko said.

"Sounds fascinating," I said, inching away from this Divine presence, "Maybe we could have lunch—at some other time—I'd like to hear all about it—actually, I've never heard of the Order of the Holy Phallus."

"Very few people have," the Reverend Meech said, "It's a little known order stemming from the Dionysiac festivals in ancient Greece, when uptight Greeks worshipped huge carved basalt penises as symbols of the generative power—followed by a potluck supper and a songfest. I felt that this Order would be just the thing for Hollywood—which was my parish at the time."

Hollywood!!!!! Suddenly I recognized this religious crock! The Polo Lounge at the Beverly Hills Hotel! Marve Fisher and I were writing a movie scenario (they used to call them) about God.

Marve and I were expert movie writers, but about God, we were a little hazy. We knew that a lot of people believed in Him so we felt there must be something to it. But then again, outside of the Bible—which was a bestseller—who could we turn to? We knew from the little research that we did at the Christian Science Reading Room—which was next to Mable's Massage Parlor on The Strip—that the Bible was mostly hearsay and had been written some 600 years after

Jesus had come down to spread the word, which, as almost everybody knows by this time, had led to quite a brush with the authorities.

Marve and I, as brash and know-it-all as we were about everything else, felt that a little technical advice about God would help us write our movie—the working title of which was "Last Tango in Galilee."

Finding a technical director among the California clergy would be a cinch—we thought. We were wrong. None of the ministers, priests, reverends, and rabbis would touch it with a ten-foot pole (which, of course, is not what we asked them). We tried to get Billy Graham (for marquee value, of course) but he was too busy with his crusades, which, upon reevaluation, was okay with us. We felt that with all those damn crusades, how the hell would he have time to dig God—which was the way Marve put it. (Great command of the language, Marve.)

We tried to get Norman Vincent Peale's unlisted telephone number with no luck at all. We called him on his listed number and his recorder answering service said, "God is everywhere, but the number you have reached is no longer in service."

The Reverend Abernathy said he was too busy with his Coppertone route (he had every black mayor in the U.S. on his list). He didn't want any of them to fade.

Marve and I had just about decided to steal a Gideon and do our own research and be our own technical advisors when we were suddenly splattered by manna from heaven.

The Polo Lounge of the Beverly Hills Hotel has always been a lucky place for me. Marve and I were sitting in an obscure booth trying to think of sorrows we could drown. We weren't having any fun except when Rona Barrett would stop at our booth and ask what's new? Each time she'd ask, we said we had been sworn to secrecy and couldn't tell her, and every time we said that Rona would spit in our drinks, which made for a pretty unsanitary afternoon and a frequent replacement of martinis.

"Maybe," Marve suggested, "maybe we should change the whole thing."

"What do you mean," I said, "change booths, or tell Rona what we know?"

"I'm talking about our movie," Marve said. "Maybe we should pick out something else. What do we know about God?"

"We didn't know anything about *The Great Gatsby,* but we wrote a great movie about it.

"Jesus," I said, "What's in these drinks anyway? We didn't write *The Great Gatsby!*"

"Well," Marve said, a beatific smile lighting up his face, "That gives us something to drink to. Hey, bartender!"

"Shhhhhhhh!"

"What's the matter? You can't talk to the bartender here?"

"It's not that. Look who just came in!"

Marve focused, almost, on the entrance to the Polo Lounge—and didn't believe it. Neither did I. There stood a man wearing a dirty white robe. We could tell right away that he was a religious man because he was carrying a seven foot cross. Something else told us that he wasn't exactly a layman—he was wearing a crown of plastic thorns instead of hair and had a few drops of plastic blood dripping down from his scalp. After checking his seven-foot cross with the hatcheck girl, he spotted Marve and me through the gloom, straightened up from his cross-carrying position, walked over, and sat down, uninvited, in the booth with us. He said nothing, which left it up to us.

"Doesn't that hurt?" I asked, indicating his crown of thorns.

"Only when I wear a beanie," he said, then, "Permit me to introduce myself. I am the Reverend Henry Meech—of the Church of the Holy Phallus."

"What?" Marve and I said together.

"Everybody always says WHAT?" the Reverend Meech said.

There could be no doubt now here in Barritos, Brazil, that this was the same Reverend Meech who started out as a simple Jesus Christ in the Polo Lounge of the Beverly Hills Hotel so many years ago.

The Reverend Meech became a large part of our life at Casa Las Bombas because he dropped in at odd hours—like three A.M. because his Honda had taken a wrong turn somewhere back in the jungle while returning home (he thought) from a rendezvous with one of his more-than-nubile converts somewhere on the mossy banks of the Amazon. The Reverend never seemed to care that the mossy banks of the Amazon usually contained alligators, anacondas, leeches, and poisonous ants. Maybe the old saying was true—God watched over drunks who lay among alligators, anacondas, leeches, and ants.

Another of our frequent religious visitors was Mahareshi Nepal, an Indian poet and guru from Bombay. He arrived in the interior of this great South American jungle country to convert the natives to Hinduism, which really confused the natives, who were being pitched at from both sides—with the Bible from the Reverend Meech and Brahmanism from Mahareshi Nepal. The desultory way Mahareshi went at his converting led me to believe he was a helluva lot more interested in his nonsequitur non-rhyming bouts with a noncommunicative muse, and in playing his Calcutta crotch bugle, a non-musical horn that is tormented into tortured sound by rhythmically squeezing one's legs together (while sitting on a bar stool) then suddenly releasing the pressure. This activates the horn. Mahareshi Nepal, we all felt, was truly a man of peace, and love, and nerve jangling dissonance.

Momomoomoo, the native and local witch doctor, is also a frequent and welcome visitor to our salon because when we had first met him on a jungle trail near our plantation, he was crouching over a smokey little fire shrinking a head and singing softly to himself "On the Good Ship Lollipop" or something that sounded very like it.

I spoke to Momomoomoo from the restaurant page in my little blue *Say-it-in-Portuguese* book, I said, "Eu não pedi isto," which means, "I did not order this." Momomoomoo did not answer me nor did he seem to notice Reiko and me at all. He might just have been all alone there in the jungle shrinking the head of someone we might know. I tried again, "Sou dos Estados Unidos (I am from the United States)."

"Fuck the United States," Momomoomoo said, rubbing the smoke out of his eyes.

"Oh," Reiko said, "He speaks English."

"Fuck the English!" Momomoomoo said. I thought I'd give it one more try so I said to him in Portuguese, (from my little blue book) "How is your family (*Como vai a sua familia?*)?"

"Fuck them, too. Say, what do you tourists want anyway? Can't-cha see I'm busy? I promised this on Tuesday, Mrs. Averback is leaving to go home to Cleveland on Tuesday. You know 'em—they live on Blue Jay Way.''

"Who's that?" Reiko said, pointing and giggling nervously at the pretty well shrunken head—"*Mr.* Averback?"

"You're smart, lady."

"Thank you," Reiko said.

"All you chinks are smart," Momomoomoo continued, "They got the army and navy stores sewed up for miles around here."

"Reiko's not a chink," I said, "She's Japanese."

"Chinks, Japanese," Momomoomoo said, "They all come from the same place. Back in 1492 the Chinese tried to find a new route to Spain, bumped square into Japan, and said 'to hell with Spain. This looks like a very nice place to raise children', so they stayed. Then they made the dumbest move they ever made. On December 7, 1941, they missed the Hilton Hotel and accidentally hit Pearl Harbor. After a couple of years of a serious misunderstanding, Harry Truman said "Drop the bomb," which they did—missing the Toyota factory and accidentally hitting Hiroshima."

Momomoomoo's version of World War II and other choice nuggets of almost information, of which he had an endless supply, helped pass the time on those steamy Brazilian nights when the television set was picking up three or four channels at the same time, and the heat lightning kept silhouetting the nearby mountains hour after hour, and jungle drums sounded like the old Buddy Rich-Gene Krupa duels, but much more ominous.

Once in awhile, Cousin Shapiro, the half Jewish, half Chinese Army-and-Navy-store owner and undercover (rumor) agent, rode out from Barritos to our place with Hurd Cambridge and his ever-pulsating wife, Elizabeth, in their Silver Cloud RR. Why Cousin Shapiro was buddy-buddy with the Cambridges was never explained. Maybe Cousin Shapiro was their private CIA. Hurd liked to keep his fingers on the pulse of the town and the economy of Brazil—*Fortune* and *Forbes* never mentioned the Brazil Nut in their endless contradictory reports about Big Business.

While Cousin Shapiro could be counted on never to get drunk, it was the contrary with Hurd and Elizabeth Cambridge. They loved their booze. Or more accurately, they loved our booze. Hurd, after the third drink started toying with some or all of Pete El Jaguar's lovely groupies. This didn't jar Pete, because it allowed him to get close to Elizabeth Cambridge and do a little toying himself. Bobby and Timothy were fascinated by all of this PG-rated carrying-on, but Parental Guidance was far from Reiko's and my intentions. It was not a matter of parental neglect; we simply felt that a little early exposure would save us all those heart-to-heart talks one is supposed to have with one's offspring when one's offspring are about to spring off.

This then was almost the extent of our social life in Barritos. It was pleasant and at times stimulating and enlightening. Despite the volume of alcohol consumed, the talk was good, and it was the first time in my life since I left Hollywood that I felt I wanted people again. Our side excursions into the Canadian bush, the Connecticut hinterlands, and the fraudulent reaches of northern Maine had all been escapes. I had become a hermit, a recluse, who only communicated with the outside world by airmail and midnight phone calls, and I had taken my little Reiko and my two ebullient children with me into limbo. Now, living here in Barritos, I grew to feel that my mode of survival in the past few years had been the wrong way to go at life. I had been running away, though I kept up a lot of energetic rearguard action, occasionally coming out of the bush, the woods, and the ice-age of Maine to let the world know (via the television book plugging expeditions) that I was still alive, well, and living, but I was a closet hermit "far from the madding crowd's ignoble strife and sales tax." Now I suddenly realized that I'd been a vegetarian going blind from too much carrot juice.

Barritos and Brazil brought me back to *this* world.

7

The condom program or "operation Killjoy" as it was known in Washington at the Agency of International Nondevelopment, was the brainchild of Congressman Harry L. Hammond of Minnesota. There had been an article in the *Reader's Digest* that really hit home with him. The article said that there were just too many people in the world and some of us would have to go. Immediately, Harry L. Hammond put down Brazil as one of the places where some must go *first!*

That night at an intimate little party in Georgetown he met Dr. Veronica Ramsey, whom he mistook for a cheerleader from the nearby college. Because, as he explained to the bartender—she looked like a cheerleader. Very bosomy and bouncey and full of pep. From the moment Harry L. Hammond met Dr. Veronica Ramsey, most of his waking hours were spent in scheming how he could get this little beauty into bed. But from all the reports I got from Senator Barry Goldwater, whom I have known since I helped him lose the presidential election, Congressman Hammond was getting nowhere rapidly with the ravishing Dr. Ramsey. The Congressman, who was married to a lovely lady who resembled John Lindsay, had six lovely children—all girls—who resembled their mother, which gives us a better understanding of The Congressman's frustrations. He finally came to realize, according to one of Barbara Howar's infrequent letters, that if he didn't cut himself loose from the almost uncontrollable, at some times, temptation of grabbing Dr. Ramsey's goodies in a public place, he'd find himself wandering down mammary lane along with Wilbur Mills, Wayne Hays, John Young, and whomever else Elizabeth Ray decides to immortalize.

Congressman Harry L. Hammond, who sure as hell didn't want to get bounced back to Duluth just yet, got his "Operation Killjoy" bill passed by sheer nagging. He then appointed Dr. Veronica Ramsey as the U.S. representative in charge, and thus made himself a hero to all those constituents back home in Minnesota by removing any danger of condoms invading Duluth. At the same time he'd get rid of the one temptation he had found himself unable to resist. Dr. Veronica Ramsey would be out of range, and Dr. Ramsey, who was really dedicated, decided that this might be the best solution to getting the Congressman off her back (figuratively and literally), and also the whole project suddenly took on the aura of a crusade. For the first time in her medical career she felt something akin to Flo Nightingale, Clara Barton and Madame Curie. And Ann Landers.

Congress passed a bill which appropriated a few billion dollars for this project. They had to cut a few billion off the project to build a dam across the Gulf of Mexico (to keep wetbacks out), and in a couple of months everything, including Doctor Ramsey and 500 cases of contraceptives, was on its way to Barritos, Brazil, which was picked as a test city by a Harris poll of the citizens of Burlington, Vermont. The poll showed that it was okay by them. Just so long as the test city wasn't Burlington, Vermont.

The arrival of Dr. Ramsey changed the character of our more or less intimate and exclusive salon. Hurd Cambridge, for one, forgot all about the local opportunities and now seemed to be devoting all of his persuasiveness to Dr. Ramsey and her Magic Mountains.

If Dr. Ramsey knew of Hurd's plans to ramjet her at the first opportunity, she showed no sign. Elizabeth Cambridge either didn't notice Hurd's elaborate persuasions or didn't care. She was usually too busy fumbling with Pete El Jaguar's fly, which required little fumbling because Pete El Jaguar, in the interest of staying the terrible onrush of time, rarely buttoned his fly, and shorts of any kind had never been part of his wardrobe.

Hurd Cambridge's first attempt to attract Veronica Ramsey into some sort of carnal alliance was made in our cozy little bar. Hurd admired a tiny heart shaped pin which Veronica wore on the slopes of her left breast. In his concupiscent eagerness he attempted to examine it more closely, by merely touching it, which resulted in having his thumb and forefinger pierced by the needle-like teeth of a tiny marmoset Veronica had been holding on her lap.

"Jesus Christ!" Hurd screamed, "I didn't know they could bite!"

"What happened, dear?" Elizabeth Cambridge wanted to know, releasing Pete El Jaguar and reaching for her tiny glass of sherry.

"Tits—with teeth!" Hurd whined, still not knowing what had happened.

"That's nice, dear," Elizabeth said, "And nothing to worry about. It's the little vampire bats we must watch out for in Barritos. They could be rabid, you know." With this Elizabeth returned to the thing at hand.

"I'm sorry," Dr. Ramsey said, shooing the marmoset back to it's perch in the rafters, "Marmosets have a tendency to be jealous."

"It is said," Mahareshi Nepal, the guru, said "The Marmoset's bite is like a message from heaven, and your lucky number is seven, or maybe eleven—or maybe even three. Only Buddha knows."

"And only I, Mahareshi," I said (I never knew whether 'Mahareshi' was his name or a title), "Only *I* know that you are a kook!"

"As Buddha said," Mahareshi continued, as though I existed only as a cardboard cutout from some theatre lobby, " 'Fly the pleasure that bites tomorrow'. . . . "

"What the hell does that mean?" Cousin Shapiro said.

"It means," Mahareshi said, "That one does not question Buddha or me, Chink!"

The night was hot, sticky, and thick with antagonisms.

Cousin Shapiro dropped his mongolian fold even lower than usual and said, quietly and inscrutably, "You, Bombay Bullshitter, son of a bitch!"

"Someday, Chink," Mahareshi said, "I will stick a Roman candle up your yellow Chinese ass and light it—"

"Look, Fellers—" I tried to intercede.

"Wait, there's more," Mahareshi said, "—and point it up your Jewish nose."

Cousin Shapiro laughed without mirth, "I'd have to be a contortionist."

"That," Mahareshi said, "can be arranged."

"Anybody like-a more tea?" Reiko asked. No one had been drinking tea since breakfast, but this was Reiko's one and only solution to any unpremeditated indelicate situation. Maybe it worked in Japan, where most of the day is spent in bowing, and muttering unspeakable oaths at each other under one's breath, but here in the steamy part of the Amazon Valley anything that stopped the forward motion and makings of a good fight was completely ignored.

Mahareshi Nepal and Cousin Shapiro stepped outside and in a few moments I heard a loud splash (the swimming pool) and shortly after that Cousin Shapiro and Mahareshi Nepal were back at the bar—toasting each other in Tequila and Tia Maria.

I went to bed. Passing the bar, I heard Cousin Shapiro say, "Fuck Bombay, Calcutta, Minneapolis and St. Paul!"

I slept like a baby.

8

Dr. Ramsey, despite her enormous personal and sexual attractiveness, was stonewalled on all sides when she tried to get both official and unofficial cooperation for her project in Barritos.

Officially, the mayor, Señor Cassares, who was running for reelection in a few years, didn't want to rock the boat by forcing condoms on a male electorate who believed that a woman's place is in the bed. The chief of police, Pancho Bocachica, accepted a gross of red, white, and blue Trojans, and said, "Very nice, very nice," then through an interpreter he asked Dr. Ramsey to take her clothes off so he could fingerprint her. After that, he'd see what he could do—officially.

Dr. Ramsey asked the interpreter to slap Pancho Bocachica's face officially, and left.

The interpreter slapped Pancho Bocachica's face, and he left, too—but much faster. Pancho Bocachica fired his crotch gun and came close to disarming himself for life.

Dr. Ramsey, hopeless as she knew the attempt would be, visited the Reverend Meech at the Rendezvous Room of his rectory. Dr. Ramsey was desperate, and she knew that he could help if he wished. The Reverend Meech was lying back on a chaise lounge dropping grapes into his mouth as he was being fanned and beaten by a handmaiden and a Pygmy with a whip. It was a new S-M team around town who called themselves "Donny and Marie."

When the Reverend Meech found out why Dr. Ramsey was there he inadvertently dropped a grape into his nose and almost suffocated.

"My dear," he said to Veronica, never taking his eyes off her tantalizing bosoms, "there is only one way you can get me to help you to convince these native savages around here to wear your little rubber gizmos—*one way*—do I make myself *clear?*"

Veronica smiled sweetly and said she understood perfectly, then she shoved a grape up his other nostril, which was still wide open, and left him gasping on the floor like a freshly caught flounder. As she slammed the rectory door, she told me, she could hear him fervently praying for a sump pump, while Donny and Marie kept on beating and fanning.

Dr. Ramsey left no possible avenue of assistance untramped— from the jungle hut of the witch doctor Momomoomoo, who volunteered to throw a couple of virgins into the volcano if it would help Mogo, Chief of the Pygmies, who was only too willing to help with the Condom Carnival, as he called it, if Dr. Ramsey would help him with a little problem he had—which seemed to be a perpetual erection, and he had been much bothered by birds landing on it. Dr. Ramsey listened to this Rogue Pygmy as he explained to her that he didn't mind sparrows, but lately he was having trouble with condors.

Dr. Ramsey knew she was getting the Pygmy put-on, but she didn't know quite how to handle it until the Mahareshi Nepal showed up to check on the present supply of virgins who enjoyed Hindu poetry. Dr. Ramsey made some quick reference to a prescription she'd write for Chief Mogo and disappeared back into the jungle.

At the end of that day, after Dr. Ramsey had exhausted all possible sources of assistance for her project, which was becoming her whole life, she dropped into the easy chair on our fan-palm-cooled patio at the Casa Las Bombas for a cold drink and a good cry, and maybe a swim.

It was almost siesta time, and Reiko had made iced tea and hot cross buns. Why hot cross buns only Reiko and St. Jude knew and St. Jude wasn't too sure, but there we were, Dr. Ramsey weeping softly as she talked out her frustrations with local conditions, Reiko and I listening sympathetically, and Bobby and Timothy, throwing, chopping and punching and crotch-kicking each other—whiling away the time until the second coming of Bruce Lee.

It seemed, Dr. Ramsey told us, that the one man in Barritos who could help her with the condom campaign was Hurd Cambridge, and he was very much against any kind of birth control, because he needed warm bodies. He needed many many field hands to pick his Brazil nuts. And he wasn't about to discourage breeding among the help.

"He's all over me—all the time," Dr. Ramsey said, dabbing at her lovely green eyes with a wispy piece of chiffon. As she sat there in a bikini that really didn't cover anything, I couldn't help thinking of the three girls in my life back in my Hollywood days that I had never made it with. This made me sad, and throb. I don't know why—the three of them must be a *mess* by *this* time.

"Why won't he help me?" Dr. Ramsey said, bending down to slip on her clogs. This movement almost popped her nipples and my mind.

"What?" I said, from somewhere on Mars.

"Why doesn't he help me convince the natives that if they don't use some preventive precaution, they'll soon eat themselves out of house and home—there just won't be enough food. Anyone with any sense at all knows that—and Hurd Cambridge knows it."

"Why," I said and sorry the moment I said it, "Why don't you give in to him. A few moments in the hay might accomplish miracles."

Dr. Ramsey looked at me. Then after a long, poignant pause, she said, "Since when is sexual intercourse any guarantee of any kind of performance of contract afterwards."

"Get the contract first."

"Men don't work like that," Dr. Ramsey said, "I know—I was a Hollywood starlet for three years before I went to UCLA medical school. Not once did I get the part. I couldn't even get a lay-on in a porno."

"What?"

"Lay-on. It's like a walk-on, except in a porno it's. . . ."

"I see what you mean," I said, quite unwillingly enlightened by Dr. Ramsey's revelations of things past.

"And that witch doctor. He could help."

"You mean Bugs Bunny?" Reiko asked.

"What?"

"Bugs Bunny. That's what I call him," Reiko explained.

"Whatever," Dr. Ramsey said, bending down again. One breast got away, the nipple pinged out and as she straightened up again, it pointed its rosy brown tip at me saying, "You! You! You!" or could it have been the jungle heat.

"Oops," Dr. Ramsey said, flipping it back in, "Sorry." I don't think she was sorry at all. I think this was all part of a little game she enjoyed playing. I was looking at Dr. Ramsey in a very different light. Maybe she wasn't all Hippocratic oath and rubber gloves and Q-tips, "scalpel, suture and sponge."

Just for the pure experimentation of the thing, I thought I'd give it a try. Merely as a scientist and researcher, and a horny rubber rancher.

The next night provided an excellent opportunity for what I had in mind. Reiko was attending a PTA meeting in Portuguese at the Barritos school and Dr. Ramsey had dropped by for some advice. I was full of it. None of this was prearranged, which no one will believe and who cares.

As soon as the tail lights of our ever-faithful little Volkswagen, which we had acquired when we lived in the Canadian bush, flicked out of sight, I started my pitch. First, of course, I mixed a couple of double martinis—using 180-proof vodka, which was like drinking on the top of Mount Olympus. One sip and Zeus struck you by lightening. One martini and you were the Flying Nun, buzzing a Russian missile site, and being fired on by BB guns loaded with nuclear warhead BBs. That was the way I felt. Dr. Ramsey had shown no sign of being bombed. She sat there like she was being cooled by the wings of butterflies. I was on fire and she was Engine Company Number 78.

The soft night air was liquid, and in the candle-bug-light her skin was pure wet gold.

"Christ!" I said, "It's hot!"

"I hadn't noticed," Dr. Ramsey said, recrossing her legs and shimmering her breasts ever so slightly under her almost seethrough blouse.

I waited until she had finished her killer-martini and asked her if she would like another. She said yes. I only made one this time. One more for *me*, and I'd forget my reason for making one for *her*.

"Aren't you joining me," she asked.

"Huh?" I managed, like a retarded cretin who had just been asked if he would like to use the bathroom instead of pissing in the corner of the living room.

"Martini—you're not having another?"

"Oh—Oh!" I said, "I had one before you came, "I'm just waiting for you to catch up."

She smiled and I said, "Christ, it's hot!"

I waited for what I, in my jumbled hurry, thought was a decent interval then I said, "Would you like to take a swim—you know— cool off????" (I *had* to *explain!*)

"I'd love to," she said. "Wow" I thought. How easy can this be???

"But I haven't," she took a large sip of her martini, "a suit."

"Oh—we're very private here—you don't—er—need a suit." Then I tried to chuckle an off-hand chuckle that came out like a Tarzan yell.

Dr. Ramsey took another slug from her martini and said, "Well, why not—" she immediately slipped out of her shoes, skirt and blouse, and there she was—just like in Penthouse! Tarzan yelled again. Suddenly we were in the pool together. She was nude. I was wearing my jungle boots, whipcord riding pants, Gaucho shirt and a jaunty (I thought) Tyrolean hat, with a cute little red and gold peacock feather. She saved me from drowning.

By the time I was breathing again, lying on the marble next to the pool, Dr. Ramsey was completely dressed and sitting in the Queen's chair we had bought from Trader Vic in Hawaii, sipping the last of her martini and puffing contentedly on a long black thin Brazilian cigar.

"Welcome home," she said, when she saw that I was conscious.

"Yeah."

9

After my near disaster I decided that even if I had drowned the whole lovely episode had been worth while. Seeing Dr. Ramsey in the buff had added ten years to my life, or maybe shortened it by twenty. It doesn't really matter. I had seen the other side of Paradise and it's even better than this side.

Dr. Ramsey, now that she knew I was no menace—which was probably the cruelest blow I had received to date—visited us at Casa Las Bombas almost daily, because almost daily she needed a shoulder to cry on.

She was getting nowhere in her condom conversion program. All the native men of Barritos accepted her little purple-boxed gifts but the condoms they contained were never worn as they were intended to be worn. Sometimes they were used as tight hats. Sometimes like rubber glove fingers, without the glove. Some of the luckier natives who had their ear lobes pierced as children to accommodate human thigh bones (they had big ears) wore the purple boxes in their ears—as I had seen the natives in Kenya wear the yellow boxes that rolls of Kodak film came in.

"I don't know what to do next," Dr. Ramsey continued, "Congressman Hammond is bound to ask questions—sooner or later."

"So what," I said, "I thought he was your boyfriend. Why would he make trouble for you?"

Dr. Ramsey flushed quickly with anger, "He's not my boyfriend. He's just a hot-pantsed small-time member of the House of Representatives from Minnesota, and how the hell he got elected is a mystery of the ages, but he takes himself very seriously—and this world overpopulation thing is the first time anybody ever listened to him about anything. And I'm supposed to be down here making it work, so he can be a hero!''

"Don't you—" Reiko said, "believe in it, too?''

"Of course I do," Dr. Ramsey said, "At first I used it as an excuse to get away from the Honorable Harry L. Hammond, United States Representative from Minnesota, 12th district, but when I got down here and saw at firsthand what overpopulation really means— those hungry little, pitiful, ragged kids hanging around the streets in Barritos, begging and. . . .''

"Well," I said, "the Honorable Harry L. Hammond has to give you some time to get the idea over. These people here barely understand anything beyond eating, drinking, and breeding, which when you come right down to it. . . .''

"When you come right down to it," Dr. Ramsey said, "You can overdo eating, drinking, and breeding.''

"What about the pill?" Reiko said, "if you can't get the men to do anything, maybe the women. . . .''

"I can't rely on the women remembering to take the pill every day," Dr. Ramsey said, "And not only that, it seems like every day they discover something else that's wrong with the pill. The side effects now have side effects. Nothing, no medication ever seems to be tested enough on humans before the drugstores are selling them by the billions. They discover that simple little remedies like No-Sleep or Sure-Sleep contain something that shortens your right leg if you use it long enough, and all we have to do to start a war with Brazil is to give their women something (if they actually take it), something that brings forth an orangutan—instead of a baby.''

"Do you think there's any chance that Congressman Hammond will come down here and check up on things?" I said.

"I certainly do think there's a good chance—anything to get away from his wife.''

"You mean the wife that looks like John Lindsay?''

"That's the one," Veronica said, "And the seven daughters who look like his wife. And if he comes down here that's going to bring on another problem besides "Operation Killjoy." In Washington, it wasn't too tough to avoid him—but here—a little torrid temperature—a few planter's punches—a big round Brazilian moon, and

I'll be wishing I was an orangutan, so I could run up a tree and out of his reach. He's going to be all over me, too.''

"Well, don't worry about that," I said, "I'll—protect you."

Reiko shrieked with laughter.

Dr. Ramsey knew why. "I think that won't be necessary," she said, "I'll just make sure the Congressman and I are never alone together. I really think I can handle the situation."

"Okay," I said, "But don't forget—Custer said the same thing."

That night, after I said my prayers and made a few additional re-requests, I lay in my little white bed thinking over the Veronica Ramsey, Rep. Harry L. Hammond situation, and it bothered me. I think most of us picture the members of our government as people of great conscience and eternal vigilance who spend all of their time making sure that our destinies are guarded and protected and that we will wind up, when it's our time, in Disneyland instead of at Forest Lawn.

In spite of all I have heard and read of the Kennedy boys misalliances with the various Hollywood availables, I just couldn't believe that they were like everybody or anybody else, and I was shocked when a recent poll asked the nation *who* did it with *JFK* and more than 60 percent of the country took one step forward.

It was like suddenly finding out that your mother did it—with your father. I refused to believe it, and I still refuse to believe that they actually did it. Can you picture your own mother and father— doing it? Of course you can't—unless you're Erica Jong (*she* could visualize the Washington Monument doing it to the Grand Canyon. And the Grand Canyon loving every minute of it).

10

The hammock, I have learned, was invented by the natives of Brazil right after they invented the siesta. Actually they invented the hammock *before* they invented the siesta, and several thousand Brazilians went stark raving mad trying to figure out what it was and how to wear it. Some wore the hammock like a hat, but it dragged a lot. Some wore it as underwear. It still dragged. Finally one day some really fastidious person washed it and hung it up to dry between two trees, and that's when the Brazilians discovered what and how to use the hammock. They'd tie it between two trees and lie down *under* it.

Nobody ever lay *in* a hammock until the white man came.

The hot, humid torpidity of the climate around Barritos was an open invitation to lie down at every opportunity. Preferably in a hammock. A great part of my life in this area was spent horizontally. I made no distinction between the siesta and any other time of the day. Any hour was fine with me, and hammock time was when I did some of my finest thinking.

It was during one of these long hours of restless repose that it came to me that if I was going to persist and/or survive in the rubber plantation business, some knowledge of what the hell rubber was all about might not be such a bad thing.

It seems that after Columbus discovered "hevea brasiliensis" as it is known to two people—me, and now you—it was first used commercially to rub out lead pencil marks, and that's how it got its name Indiarubber. Later shortened to just "rubber." This sounds so simple that it sounds like I made it up—but I didn't—it's all there in *Funk and Wagnalls,* and what I couldn't find in books I learned from our plantation foreman, Mr. Claudio. Mr. Claudio spoke English more or less—more than a treetoad and less than Charo.

Mr. Claudio could have told me a lot more about rubber but it would have had to be in Portuguese and that would be a waste of time because the longer we stayed in Brazil the more Portuguese sounded like Spanish—as it is spoken at the Warsaw Holiday Inn.

The few words I knew in Portuguese were enough to make myself misunderstood by everyone in Barritos. And the only words I knew in the local Indian language were "Coca-Cola." So instead of saying *arrivederci* or *aloha,* or *ciao,* we'd say "Coca-Cola" and everyone seemed to understand. Besides, communication didn't seem very important compared to other problems such as trying to sell my rubber. Selling rubber, grown two thousand miles upriver from Belém, the only port that any commercial tramp steamer bothered with, was almost an impossibility. There was no such thing as making our rubber into little balls and bouncing them down to Belém. Our rubber was made into enormous smoked balls that could barely be rolled—let alone bounced—but that's the way the natives had been processing the sticky latex that dribbled from our thousands of trees for the past eighty or more years. The Barritos natives had no idea of the connection between our thousands of gummy pails of latex milk and the tightly rolled little rubber objects which Dr. Ramsey was dispensing to them by the gross, and which they used as funny little balloons to be blown up until they burst with a loud, funny pop. They thought the condoms were more in the bubblegum category and not in their wildest dreams did they suspect that the stuff they were milking from our rubber trees would ever come back to them in the form of goalies in the mating game.

"You know, Mr. Douglas," Claudio said to me in Pidgin-Portuguese one humidity-saturated day as we strolled at a very slow rate along a row of rubber trees, sweating almost enough to irrigate them, "You know, we got a very good crop this year—almost four hundred pounds per acre."

"Good news," I said, like I had just heard about the San Francisco earthquake. "What are we gonna do with it?"

"Send it to Belém."

"How?"

"My grandfather, he owns the good ship *Lola Falana*. We just load the big balls on the deck—shove off, and in a week, we'll be in Belém."

"I like that, Claudio," I said, "I like that very much. But what happens when we get to Belém?"

"What always happens to anybody who first gets to Belém. We get drunk at the Café Gloria."

"I like that, too," I said. "But what about the rubber balls—the big rubber balls. We gotta get rid of them!"

This slowed Claudio down but not for very long. "You're gonna like the Café Gloria," he said. "You ever got drunk there?"

"No," I said. "I never even heard of the Café Gloria. The first and last time I was in Belém all I did was change planes for Manaus—you know, Manaus—it used to be the rubber capital of the world. They also got a big fancy opera house, and once, a couple of years ago, Danny Kaye irritated a lot of little under-privileged children there. He goes all over the world doing that."

Caludio wasn't interested in Manaus or Danny Kaye. He was only interested in the booze at the Café Gloria, and after he talked for a while longer, I was beginning to feel the same way.

"How do you know you can sell the rubber in Belém or whatever?" Reiko wanted to know.

"What do you think I'm gonna do," I said, "sail two thousand miles down the river on a chance that I'm gonna be able to sell my rubber? I'm gonna write and find out first!"

"Write?" Reiko said, "write to whom?" She was so practical.

"How the hell do I know?" I said. "Somebody in the rubber business. Firestone, Goodrich, Goodyear, Henry Kissinger. How do I know who? I gotta find out *who*!"

"Henry Kissinger is not in the rubber business!"

"How do *you* know?"

"I read all about him in the *Tokyo Shimbum* (which is the Japanese *Village Voice*). He doesn't have time to be in the rubber business. Everyday he flies back and forth between Israel and Egypt."

"Why?"

"Because they both keep telling him to get the hell out, that's why!" (I didn't think she knew.)

I'll never forget the Café Gloria because when Claudio and I arrived there we couldn't find it, so we settled for "The Hole of the Howler Monkey," another café or saloon that was slightly lower in social tone (I assumed from Claudio's description of the former) and catered to cave persons only. Claudio and I were the only patrons with foreheads. We stood out embarrassingly, though after a few Banzai BoomBooms (a drink made from frozen sneaker juice with a dash of vermouth and drunk through a perforated green banana), I didn't care and started to sing "Down By the Old Mill Stream" at the top of my lungs. "Better slow down—those drinks—they'll knock you on your camasitza!" Claudio said. Camasitza turned out to be the Portuguese word for contusãu. Which is worth knowing and may stand you in good stead if you're ever in the Hole of the Howler Monkey in Belém, Para, Brazil. Flat on your camasitza.

Claudio was right, after three Banzai BoomBooms I didn't care if we sold our boatload of rubber balls or not. For awhile there we were seriously considering going back on board and pitching our whole cargo into the silted muck of the Belém harbor and watch it float the sixty miles or so downriver and into the Atlantic, but we soon got over this very intelligent thought when we saw Gertrude and Carmenita. Gertrude and Carmenita were hookers (what else in a cave person bar?), and they thought Claudio and I were *cute* and we should buy *them* a drink because we were.

After several more Banzai BoomBooms (who counts after the first ten?), Claudio and I thought Gertrude and Carmenita were Candy Bergen and Hugh Hefner. I was entranced by Candy and Claudio was hooked on Hugh—until two local cave dwellers sat down with us at our rickety bamboo table and changed our plans completely.

It was *then* we went back to the dock and our good ship *Lola Falana* and dumped our whole cargo into the outgoing tide. I must say it floated real nice and we got a great hand from the crowd lining the rail when the last of the latex hit the bay.

Two days later I was back in Barritos courtesy of Varig and two bush planes and their flaky pilots (upside down was just as good as right side up to them), who missed rock-nobbed mountains and sheer granite cliffs by centimeters. They'd go down to skim the greeny river and scare Indian filled canoes into splashy panic as they'd all start paddling in opposite directions. Another spectacular trick was to leap the thundering waterfalls like salmon—barely missing the top outcroppings of knife-edged basalt.

I thought, My God! I'll never live to see Mary Tyler Moore again! But somehow, through just plain bad luck (the pilot's), we didn't hit a thing and suddenly the Barritos airport was bumping under our Piper Cub wheels and we slurped to a stop in a swampy part of the field. The swampy part of the Barritos airfield was full of anacondas, where they lurked hoping to grab off a tasty black caiman alligator as the caimans also hung around the swamp in groups. Which meant there really wasn't too much of a choice—in the air, or on the ground, fatality was almost guaranteed.

The reception I got from the overseer (Reiko) of the Casa Las Bombas wasn't exactly what Lindbergh got when he landed in Paris in 1927. Reiko had an overweening desire to know where the money was for our rubber crop and when I finally told her the whole story (leaving out Gertrude and Hefner), she started packing for Japan.

When I explained that the price of rubber had dropped because the Chinese were making a cheaper grade in Taiwan and Hong Kong, Reiko said she'd buy that, but what happened to our almost 180 tons of unprocessed rubber balls!

I told her I had given them to a little old lady who needed them worse than we did. She didn't buy that and started packing for Japan again.

Along about the third day of intermittent warfare Reiko had a long talk with Dr. Ramsey, and whatever Dr. Ramsey told her she forgave me, and Dr. Ramsey told me never to tell any woman the truth. The truth, she said, always sounds too illogical to a woman. A wild, crazy, insane lie is better and always makes sense to the female psyche.

"Words to Live By."

11

The episode of the jettisoned rubber balls was forgotten, and the business of earning some daily bread continued. The Brazilian rubber business being what it was I wrote several columns for a newspaper syndicate in Chicago. It was fun being a columnist. I could cut loose with all my gripes, in a charmingly amusing way and get paid for it. Before this I used to write eight-page letters to my defenseless friends in California.

After a visit to the Barritos post office to mail the columns—murmuring a little prayer that they'd make the afternoon mail plane and that the afternoon mail plane, please God, would not hit the mountain—I arrived back at the ranch heavy with protein-enriched perspiration and decided on a swim before dinner. This turned out to be not such a good idea. Bobby and Timothy, home from school, joined me, and we had a jolly frolic in the luke-warm pool sans, of course, bathing suits.

We were just about to leave the pool for a brisk rubdown with a damp (the only kind we ever had in this climate) towel, when we heard a weird sound. I thought it was a couple of jaguars or some other big jungle cats fighting. We knew there were jaguars around, but never much in the daylight and also never so close to the house.

Bobby, Timothy, and I were hanging on the edge of the pool—listening.

"What is it, Papa?" Timothy wanted to know.

"It's cats," Bobby said, "Big cats!"

"I would say so," I agreed, having no idea whether I was right or wrong.

"They're fighting," Bobby said.

"What about?" Timothy said. "Maybe," I said, "over a piece of meat or another cat—if they're males."

"Why do they have to be *males*?" Timothy said.

"Because, Dumbo," Bobby said, "Males always fight over a piece of meat or a female."

"*You're* Dumbo," Timothy said, and gave up.

The strange screeching and screaming turned out to be something quite different than we theorized. This is putting it very mildly. Again Bobby and Timothy and I were about to hoist ourselves out of the swimming pool and into the house when the big iron gate which leads to our hacienda opened and four Scottish bagpipers swung through—marching with the typical measured and exact step that all Scottish bagpipers seem to be born with. It had rhythm but it was the rhythm of programmed robots that you know would never vary if they were made to march through a forest fire or a field of molten lava.

"It ain't cats," Bobby said.

"What those things they're sucking on?" Timothy wanted to know.

"Bagpipes," I said. I felt I should.

"Cats would sound better," Timothy said, not knowing that he had just insulted every Scotsman who had ever lived. I agreed with him, but having once marched in a parade in Glasgow with some Scottish pipers, I knew that their seemingly monotonous beat was the greatest marching beat in the world. The pipers had saved many a British army from retreating in disorder after a disastrous battle, and had also restored the vitality of an exhausted regiment during the last five miles of a thirty-mile enforced hike. The beat of the pipers was the beat of the heart.

Bobby and Timothy and I had forgotten we were naked in our pool, when we suddenly saw behind the small group of pipers, two plumed and shining black horses (which, I learned later, had been borrowed from the Barritos Undertaking and Alligator Tanning Company). The horses were plumed with wild jungle-bird tails and they were pulling a golden coach.

"Holy Jesus, Mary, and what's-his-name!" Bobby said.

"What is it, Papa?" Timothy asked.

"I don't know," I said. "But they sure got the wrong house."

"I know who it is," Bobby said. "It's the Avon Lady and she's been smoking pot."

"Yes," Timothy said, "—pot."

By this time the driver of the golden coach, who turned out to be Pete El Jaguar, the bandit, reined in his two shiny-black horses and the golden coach groaned to a stop.

Pete, with more alacrity than I had ever seen him exhibit before, bounced to the ground and opened the golden door of the golden coach. Out came a queen, who immediately missed the three steps and landed in a large strewn-out mess on our lawn. Her crown rolled off her head and into the deep end of the swimming pool.

Pete El Jaguar forgot he was an attendant of the queen and roared with dirty Portuguese laughter. The queen had to pick her own self up because Pete was too overcome.

The queen slapped Pete's face and he immediately quieted down, and I thought he was going to slap her right back but he controlled himself.

"You forget," roared the queen, "I am the queen and you are but a humble peasant!" Pete El Jaguar agreed with this—too quickly, I thought.

"Where the fuck is my crown?" the queen said, looking around our patio through a monstrous very dull and very cracked lorgnette. It was then we all recognized her. The "queen" was the Reverend Meech's wife, and high on something (if not pot).

"I'll get it," Bobby whispered and dove down into the deep end.

"Where are your clothes?" The queen had spotted us at the pool.

"Oh," I said, hanging onto the pool side with one hand, "we're just peasants—we're too poor to buy clothes—all we have to wear is our skin—which we get from the government with skin stamps."

The queen thought about this for a long moment, then she laughed.

"My," she said, "that's droll—really droll—you are a really droll fellow, and I shall have your head removed at my earliest convenience."

"Here's your crown, Lady." Bobby said handing it up to Mrs. Meech, who took and placed it high upon a pile of mousey brown hair, which looked like it had been combed by a knife and fork.

"Thank you, Dear Boy," the queen said. "My you ARE a boy aren't you?"

Bobby, who was just coming into the age of exhibitionism, said, "yes" and floated on his back. He looked like a pink submarine with very limber periscope.

"Bobby," I said, "you don't have to prove anything—yet."

"I hope not," Bobby muttered. "Not with that old bag, anyway."

"Well," Mrs. Meech said, "I must be off—" and started back to her golden coach (which in between royalty carried stiffs to the Barritos cemetery). Mrs. Meech, the queen, repeated herself, "I must be off—"

Why did she have to say it *twice,* I wondered.

"I think she's just lonely," Reiko said later, while we were having dinner on the patio by the light of the largest moon I have ever seen just rising above the rubber and palm trees. It made us all look like we were made of orange gold.

"That's pretty lonely," I said. "Driving all over town making out like she's the queen."

"She didn't say 'queen' of what country," Bobby said.

"Scotland," Timothy said, surprisingly.

"Scotland doesn't have a queen," Bobby said with an accompanying sneer.

"They do now," Timothy, sneering right back. Such loving brothers. Cain and Abel rise again..

"What's she lonely about?" I asked.

"That horny husband of hers," Reiko said, making me wonder where she had picked up "horny"—certainly not from me. "All he does is go around all day and half the night trying to 'convert' as many young native girls as possible."

"What does 'convert' mean?" Bobby asked.

"Screw," Timothy answered.

"He's never home," Reiko tried to divert the conversation.

"Screw!" Timothy repeated somewhat louder.

"Timothy," I said, "little boys don't use that word."

"I'm seven and a half going on eight," Timothy said. "Screw!"

"But why," Reiko said, still trying, "why does she think she's the queen of England—or wherever?"

"Well," I said, "from all appearances—maybe she's got a screw loose."

"Screw," Timothy said.

"Timothy," I said, "we heard you the first 17 times—you didn't get a laugh then—so give up—you'll never get a laugh now."

"I like the queen," Timothy said, "and I like that gold wagon—it's real cool."

"Timothy—why don't you go down to the swamp and see if you can find an anaconda."

"I found one this morning."

"Good," I said, "go play somewhere."

"It's under the table right now."

The table was evacuated like we were all shot from guns at the puffed-rice factory in Battle Creek. And sure enough (my kids aren't liars), there was a large box under the table, just full of anaconda. He was only about seven or eight feet long and seemed pretty happy when Reiko gingerly released him from his box.

"Timothy," I said, "where did you get that anaconda? You didn't catch him yourself and put him in that box."

"Papa, you've got to believe me. I caught him all by myself. I got a little turtle and I put him in that box, then I put the box down by that big mudhole in the swamp and pretty soon that big snake got into the box after the turtle and I closed the lid on him and dragged him home."

"Where's the little turtle?" Bobby said.

"Where's the snake?" Timothy said.

"He's gone."

"Well," Timothy said, "find the snake and you'll find the turtle."

The bell outside our iron gate clanged and Reiko went to see who it was. It was the Reverend Meech.

"Ah there, Reverend," I said, "what do you hear from the Pope?"

"Nothing," the Reverend Meech said, "absolutely nothing. We Lutherans or whatever we are very seldom get any messages from his Holiness. Pope John, actually, was the last Pope who talked to us at all."

"Well," I said, "Pope John was one of the boys. He was a regular one. He came up through the ranks."

"My father's a Buddhist priest," Reiko said (which is true). "Pope John used to write to him in Japanese—all the time."

"Wait a minute," I said, before the Reverend Meech could get started on this. "Why? How come Pope John used to write to your father all the time?"

"Because," Reiko said, "my father also was a Toyota dealer and Pope John wanted to trade in his Fiat."

"If," I said, "if I believe *that* I'll believe anything."

Reiko pouted for the next half hour.

"I am here," the Reverend Meech announced after the third or fourth scotch and water, "looking for my wife—" then he added, "Queen Elizabeth."

"Oh," Reiko said, "sorry to hear about Margaret and Tony—I mean the split up. They seemed like such a nice couple."

"Who?" said the Reverend Meech. Maybe he'd had more than three or four scotches.

"Forget it," Reiko said.

"Screw!" Timothy said.

"Oh, that reminds me," the Reverend Meech said. "I must be going. Gotta pick up a fifth of holy water, some wine, and wafers at the A&P. Nice seeing you folks again, and if you see the Queen—"

"Yes?" I said.

"You didn't see *me*," the Reverend Meech said and was gone— like he hadn't really been there at all.

12

Dr. Ramsey's "Crusade for Contraception" was still going nowhere, and she had to ask the U.S. Government for more condoms. Five hundred crates more. While some of the original supply had been used as they were intended, most of the condoms which had come in all colors (the brainchild of somebody at U.S. Rubber or wherever) were utilized as party decorations, engagement rings, or weather balloons at the Barritos airport control tower (which had nothing to do with controlling the landing of aircraft). The Barritos airport control tower had been built when the Barritos airfield was just a swamp. What was now called the control tower was actually a duck-blind built for shooting ducks and egrets. The egret feathers were in great demand at the turn of the century as decoration on M'lady's hats, which didn't do much for M'lady's hat, and even less for the egrets. When it was discovered that there were only three families of egrets left, the government acted quickly (they always act quickly three days after it's too late) and placed a ban on the killing of egrets.

Likewise the Barritos airfield weather balloon project was just more political nonsense, but it did keep the local weatherman—who for years thought a barometer was just a clock that ran backwards and forwards and didn't make any tick-tocks—busy blowing up colored condoms to let them fly away into the stratosphere. He never knew why. It was a job.

Dr. Ramsey, despite her many setbacks and disappointments, never seemed to be really discouraged, although I'm sure she was—she wasn't made of stone. *What* she was made of I never dared again to find out.

* * *

Every once in a while tourists from either Lindblad Tours or Dick Brill's "Green Hell" Tours got separated from the main group and showed up at our Casa Las Bombas, just as it seemed they were about to draw their last breath of the almost unbreathable (some days) air—it was so humid. When this first started to happen and these people stumbled into our patio, I thought they were zombies who needed new batteries, or a good jolt courtesy of Dr. Frankenstein.

Mr. and Mrs. Tooze were a couple of these lost-sheep tourists. Mr. and Mrs. Chester Tooze were the unlikeliest couple I have ever known. They wandered in one afternoon just as we had all settled down for a two-hour siesta, and a two-hour siesta in that climate wasn't enough.

Mr. and Mrs. Tooze rang our gate bell—insistently, or I would have ignored it. But after almost a half hour of clang! clang! my curiosity was aroused to the point of justifiable homicide. I fell out of my hammock and staggered over to the gate, almost de-skulling myself on an unseen rake, which flipped up and whacked my forehead with such a resounding "*zonk!*" that my whole life flashed before me—plus a couple of short subjects, a Donald Duck, and a Lowell Thomas Remembers. I don't know how long this took but Mr. and Mrs. Tooze waited.

When I opened the locked gate Mrs. Tooze explained, unnecessarily, that her husband, who she nudged toward me, was related in some way to the famous Mrs. Tooze, whom we all know and love as head of the Women's Christian Temperance Union. This thrilled me beyond words, but before I could ring for a servant to bring me a few rabid bats to let loose in the direction of our would-be guests, I thought, what the hell, they're just poor tourists and I'm the only St. Bernard within miles, so I invited them inside.

"Who is it?" Reiko wanted to know from her comfortable hammock strung out between the roots of a huge Banyan tree.

"It's Mr. and Mrs. Tooze," I said.

"Banzai!" Reiko said and turned over and faced the jungle in back of her.

"Nice place you've got here," Mr. Tooze ventured, "Lotta trees."

"Yeah," I said. "We gotta have a lotta trees—rubber, you know."

Mrs. Tooze started to laugh. She must have weighed almost three hundred pounds and when she started to laugh, a few loose stones fell down from the wall around the swimming pool.

"Did I say something?" I wanted to know.

"Yeah," Chester Tooze said, "Minerva here thinks it's funny— you know—trees made out of rubber—when you could have real ones."

"Wait a minute," I started.

"What about them bananas over there," Mrs. Tooze said, "they rubber, too?"

"No," I said. "But you can't eat them. . . ."

"Plastic?"

"No. They're green. That's why you can't eat them," I said, wishing to Christ I had not opened the gate.

By this time, Reiko had turned back to the tableau taking place in our very private patio, and Bobby and Timothy were wide awake. Siesta, it seemed, was over.

"Would you like-a tea?" Reiko asked, suddenly becoming the perfect Japanese wife, which she hadn't practiced being for a long long time (with me, anyway).

"That would be very nice," Mrs. Tooze said, and giggled a little, which loosened a few more little rocks. Mrs. Tooze with her immense size (encased, by the way in a Hawaiian muu-muu) had about thirty-five pounds of bright red hair. From the distance, I imagined, she looked like a volcano being born in a Mexican corn field—like Paricutín.

Mr. Tooze, or Chet, as I surmised he had been called at every Rotary Club from Bangor, Maine, to Bali, was about seven feet tall and looked like the center on the basketball team from the City of Hope. Chet didn't have red hair, but he had a neck that had spent most of its life facing the sun from the top of a wheat harvester in Kansas. Either that or he had it tinted at Westmore's.

We finally, during tea, got through to Chet and Minerva that we were running a rubber plantation and all those trees out there were leaking latex day and night—and making us poor. They didn't get the humorous intent of this last so I gave up. I should have given it up years ago, joking with the laymen, but I never learned.

"I looked it up," Bobby suddenly said, with a mouthful of bread and jam and peanut butter and honey and brown sugar. To understand him was the trick of the year, but I let him go on. I even encouraged him with "You looked WHAT up?"

"Mrs. Tooze's name—Minerva—it means goddess of plenty."

I looked at Mrs. Tooze expecting an unhappy reaction but she laughed down a few more loose rocks (larger this time) from our poolside wall and said, "Bobby—or whatever your name is—you're so right. I've got plenty for everybody. That's what Mr. Tooze says. Right, Chet?"

Chet was too busy staring at one of our Indian girl helpers who was pouring the tea. Our Indian girl helper was topless for no other reason than pure custom and the fact that most of them had beautiful bosoms (as they used to be called back in the U.S.).

Mrs. Tooze repeated her question and Chet's answer was merely, "Huh?"

I asked him sometime later if he'd like to see some rubber trees at work and got the same slack-mouthed answer.

Mrs. Tooze's given name may have meant the goddess of plenty to Bobby (and incorrectly so), but once the natives, Indians, and half-breeds of Barritos got a quick scan of her warping through the narrow streets of their town she somehow got to be known almost overnight as the "Goddess of Fertility." I suspected that this was the work of Dr. Ramsey, who was finally getting so tired of the runarounds and other tricky devices used against her by the various opponents of the All-American condom, that she started her own little garden of deviousness. Dr. Ramsey had plans for this newly arrived "Goddess." One Tuesday night under the guise of music and entertainment at the once-resplendent Barritos opera house, the good Doctor arranged to present Carlos Ramada and his Banana Bunch (as Carlos called his marimba and oil drum band) along with a few songs by the local Yma Sumac who was really Amy Camus from

Brooklyn—plus a short course in the use of the condom by the "Goddess of Fertility" (this last was not announced too prominently).

The big night was a success—a brilliant success. Carlos Ramada and his band never sounded worse, and in seventeen songs Amy Camus missed the key by a tone and a half in all but one. And the people of Barritos crowded the ancient opera house so full that the walls breathed.

Mrs. Chester Tooze, the headline, was a smash. She demonstrated before an audience who reacted to her like she was Mick Jagger and when she showed them, with the aid of a long wooden broom handle, just how the condom should be adjusted—then waved it back and forth as in the motions of surrender—the crowd went absolutely stark raving mad.

Minerva tried to explain (as coached by Dr. Ramsey) above the din that this little device on the end of the broom handle, if used properly, would *increase* fertility. No one heard her at first but after a while the happily wild rioting mob quieted down, for just a moment, and listened. Then they went berserk again—cheering, screaming, squealing, yelling, wailing, waa-hooing, screeching, beating each other with dishpans, bongo drums, and small children. Pandemonium! PAN-DE-MO-NIUM!!!!

The next day there wasn't a broom handle to be had anywhere from São Paulo to the Venezuela border. The "Goddess of Fertility" had done her work well.

13

It was very early in the morning. It had to be early in the morning because the climate of Barritos became catastrophic at any time beyond 10:00 A.M. Not only was it hot, the air was liquid. I'm sure the longer we lived there the more we were developing gills.

Reiko and Dr. Ramsey, her chest, and I were at Cousin Shapiro's Army & Navy store to buy some Levis.

We had heard (through the grapevine or jungle coconut telegraph) that Cousin Shapiro was a double-agent, which sounded very ominous, but as it turned out, he was. He sent regular reports to Peking, written, of course, in Chinese, on the underside of large crates of Brazil nuts. These reports he culled from the *National Geographic* and by the time they got to the Chinese government the reports on the conditions in Brazil could be months or even years old. Cousin Shapiro knew that they wouldn't know this and also that probably no one in Peking would have access to the *National Geographic*.

The other side of his double-agenting was a bit more serious, but all he could ever offer, really, were suspicions. Cousin Shapiro was reasonably sure (in his work for the Israeli government) that Mr. Brown (Braun?) was really Wolfgang Bucholtzer, the notorious Nazi art thief who had grabbed millions of dollars worth of Jewish art in Europe and U-boated it to South America. Cousin Shapiro had never seen any of this art. It was impossible to approach Mr. Brown's fancy plantation house way back in the bush because it was surrounded by wall-to-wall Doberman-Pinschers (who had their teeth filed to points).

"How's my favorite double-agent-spy-Army and Navy Store proprietor," I asked Cousin Shapiro as we entered his darkened, delicious (he also sold Oriental delicacies), denim den.

"Fine," Cousin Shapiro said, "you like to buy a German field-marshal uniform? Special today. But you gotta show your Nazi ID card. And only one field-marshal uniform to a customer."

"I just want a pair of faded blue demins," Dr. Ramsey said, "and real tight."

"I know what you mean," Cousin Shapiro said. "And I will personally see to it that they are real tight. I'll fit them *myself.*"

"You can try," Dr. Ramsey said, "but you may wind up with a couple-a broken lichee nuts, and I'll see that you get mouth-to-mouth resuscitation with a tidy bowl plunger."

"And you, Mrs. Douglas," Cousin Shapiro said, "what can I do for you—some nice nori (Japanese seaweed)?"

"No," Reiko said, "today I want taco!"

"I don't know how you can eat that stuff," Cousin Shapiro said, "Octopus—Ugh!"

"Chinese people eat octopus all the time," Reiko said.

"I'm half Jewish," Cousin Shapiro said.

"What's the matter," Dr. Ramsey said. "Can't you get a rabbi to kill an octopus?" Which I thought was pretty funny—for a girl with big boobs. (They usually are not very bright. Those things drain their brains.)

"Look, Mr. Shapiro," Dr. Ramsey said, "I'm in trouble."

"I shouldn't wonder," Cousin Shapiro said, admiring her unbelievable superstructure. "Be impossible to avoid."

"You don't understand," Dr. Ramsey said.

"I'm not *that* old, Doctor!" Cousin Shapiro said.

"How am I going to stop all this overpopulation," Dr. Ramsey said, "don't these people understand that in a few years there won't be any room for them? Even here in the jungle there won't be any food—there won't be any—anything—including breeding! They won't be able to move. What do they think they'll be able to do if there is no room to do it in???"

Cousin Shapiro lowered his eyes to her bustline and moved them from side to side like he was watching a tennis match between two pregnant woodchucks before he answered.

"Unbelievable," he said. He had forgotten the question entirely.

"Of course, it is," Dr. Ramsey said. "How can they be so short-sighted as not to see things getting worse every day."

"I wouldn't say so," Cousin Shapiro said, his almond lidded eyes resting once again on Dr. Ramsey's "priceless pair," as Hurd had once called them. The whole episode was developing into a pretty cheap double entendre dependence on Dr. Ramsey's tuberosity, which she either ignored or had not noticed. Either way, I felt we must end it or we'd never get what we came for, which was Levis for all.

"Look," I said, "haven't we had enough fun with Dr. Ramsey's boobies for a while—why don't we—" There was a silence—

"I wasn't mindful of anyone having fun with my—" Dr. Ramsey stopped and I felt she was about to leave the vicinity.

"Wait a minute," I said. "Please—I—I—it just slipped out, but, Dr. Ramsey, you must know that, well you are—are—"

"Built like a brick pagoda," finished Cousin Shapiro.

Dr. Ramsey blushed—deeply. "I suppose—" she started, "but I guess I'm so used to—look, I came here to buy a pair of Levi's and that's what I want—twenty-two waist, size eight, and very faded—"

"Don't worry," Reiko said, "two days in this Amazon sun and they'll be white." She fanned herself vigorously with one of the two dozen Japanese fans her mother had sent her from Japan, when she first learned we were moving to this region. The Japanese, who long ago migrated, by invitation, know more about Brazil than they do about the U.S.

Cousin Shapiro suddenly became all business, as all business as he was capable, sitting curled up in *his* Queen Liliuokalani chair that Don The Beachcomber had sent him from Hollywood many ears before, in exchange for some Chinese balls (glass).

Cousin Shapiro did not rise from his B'nai B'rith lotus position, but he pointed to a dark corner where in the dim, I could make out, I think, a pants rack. Dr. Ramsey and Reiko moved off in that direction while I stayed with Cousin Shapiro hoping to learn "what's up?"

"What's up?" I said, very casually.

"That's not very casual," Cousin Shapiro said. "If you are looking for information about my present activities—which of course are deeply secret."

"You're not going to *leak* anything—like on the six o'clock news?" I said, disappointed, but ready.

"You mean about Reichmarshal Braun and his storm troopers drilling out there in the jungle every day at two P.M.?"

"You mean, during siesta?" I was astonished. Brown or Braun must have been *very* serious—or frothing mad. No one or nothing moved between twelve noon and four P.M. in Brazil.

"That was quite a leak," I said. "I knew nothing about that."

"How could you," Cousin Shapiro said. "You don't speak the language."

"I don't hafta speak the language," I said. "What's to understand about a lot of Krauts drilling out in the jungle?"

"They're not Krauts," Cousin Shapiro patiently started to explain. "They're Brazilians, Indians, Mestizos, anybody who lives around here. Like I saw Claudio there."

"Claudio? My foreman? Drilling with the Krauts? What for? They gonna start something? Like World War III?"

"They got a lot of new weapons."

"Maybe they know somebody in the IRA," I said. "*They* probably have a surplus by now—with all the help they've been getting from Bingo games all across the U.S."

"You're kidding!" Cousin Shapiro said, not at all surprised or bestirred.

"I don't know for sure," I said. "All I know is what I read in the *National Enquirer*."

"What do *they* know?" Cousin Shapiro said.

"*Everything.*"

"How do I look?" Dr. Ramsey said, whirling around in front of Cousin Shapiro and me.

Dr. Ramsey's new Levi's were pasted on her. I don't see how she even had room for her skin. They couldn't have been any tighter if she wore them *under* it.

"They're a little loose here," Cousin Shapiro said, smoothing Dr. Ramsey's right buttock. I don't know how he did it. He was ten feet from her.

"Yeah," Dr. Ramsey agreed, "but they'll shrink, or I'll just bend over a lot. Know what I mean, dirty old Chink?"

"Diry old *Jewish* Chink," Cousin Shapiro corrected her.

14

I found it difficult to believe in almost everything that Cousin Shapiro told me about anything. He had large bottles of ground rhino horn stacked on his shelves in the pharmaceutical section of his Army & Navy store. This nostrum, according to Buddha, Cousin Shapiro told me, was the Bergdorf Goodman of aphrodisiacs and came in three strengths: "Strong," "Very Strong!" and "Heaven Help the Working Girl—Especially if she's working Eighth Avenue or Forty-second Street."

When I asked him why he was selling aphrodisiacs in a neighborhood where copulation was second only to Pepsi, he said, "Because everybody has to believe in something."

"What about God?" I said. "Don't they believe in Him?"

"This is a Catholic country," he said. "They hafta!"

I really had no idea where this conversation was going but I learned that ground-up rhino horn was a very popular item in Barritos, so much so that Cousin Shapiro couldn't keep enough of it in stock, which may have contributed to Dr. Ramsey's problem—anybody with a kilo of ground-up rhino horn wasn't going to let it go to waste.

Cousin Shapiro's opium inspired (and I'm just guessing because he's Chinese—I don't know what the Jews smoke) and fanciful tale of Mr. Brown drilling an army back in the jungle remained just one of thousands of rumors that came over the coconut telegraph every day in and around Barritos, until the fateful day I rounded a bend on an old footpath which ran alongside a pleasant little jungle stream, which was infested by leeches and mosquitoes, which carried sleeping sickness, malaria, and yellow fever from village to village.

I really wasn't watching just where I was stepping, and I tripped over a huge snapping turtle who managed to wake up just long enough to tear off one of my Keds. He missed my whole foot by a hair and looked pretty disgusted. I guess it made him feel old.

When I looked up I heard a shout: "Achtung!" and there *they* were and there *he* was—Field Marshal Braun dressed in a World War I officer's uniform complete with polished boots, an iron cross at his throat, and a spiked helmet on his head. His right hand held a vicious sword, and his left, a pair of white gloves. He looked quite nutty, but quite dangerous, and his shouting would have put the fear of the fatherland into the most reluctant draft-dodging Kraut.

The army he was drilling was something else. It included, as Cousin Shapiro had reported, my foreman, Claudio, who was dressed in a uniform which was part Swiss guard, part Gilbert and Sullivan, and part Goodwill Industries. he looked like a mercenary who was being paid to crush a revolt of Radio City Rockettes.

Field Marshal Braun was trying to teach a motley crew of about fifty local Barritosians some sort of close order drill which resembled the course given to Tokyo subway guards on how to pack a one-hundred seat subway car with two thousand people in three seconds, and still have time left for a smoke.

The whole thing looked like choreographed chaos. "Left face! Right face! About face and forward haaaaaarch!" This confused group seemed to believe all these commands had to be obeyed *simultaneously*. Not *one* military movement at a time. The result led to an overwhelming abundance of bumping, elbowing, and accusatory scowlings. This was an army which *should* have been traveling on its stomach. Progress would have been slower but a helluva lot neater.

I took what I felt to be the necessary precaution of remaining out of sight of the Field Marshal and his fun-loving troops. The more fun-loving they became with their weird technique of military maneuvering, the more they giggled until finally the whole troop was screaming with laughter and their Field Marshal was almost apoplectic with frustration. His Babel of German, Portuguese, and Amerindian bellowings only served to increase the "inharmonious harmony" and confusion. It was bedlam at its best.

Deciding that a cautious retreat would be the thing to do, I backed up along the narrow path. The snapping turtle got the other Ked and I got the hell out of there as quickly as my bare feet would let me. I felt that if the Field Marshal had spotted me, the excuse of a live target might have united his ragged troop into something resembling a posse, and I would have discovered the thrill of the chase without benefit of the rules set by the Humane Society to prevent excessive cruelty to the fox at the Brookville Hunt Club.

Replacing my Keds at Cousin Shapiro's Army and Navy Store, I told him the story. Cousin Shapiro carefully spun the dial, opened a large wall safe, removed several ledgers from it, and spread them on the counter.

"Now," he said. "How many did you say Brown had in his troop?"

"Wait a minute," I said. "I don't want to get mixed up in any local politics or local anything. I had enough of that up in Maine. Anything local you can have."

"This isn't local," Cousin Shapiro was being patient. "This Nazi bastard has something in mind. Like taking over Barritos."

"What the hell would he do with it? Barritos, it's over the hill. Barritos' days of glory are gone forever. What would the Nazis do with it?"

"What did they do with Prague? That's what everybody said when they moved in on Prague. Who cares? Who needs Prague? Let 'em have it. Let 'em have fun. Then next it was Poland, Russia, France, and on and on, and then we had little incidents like the bombing flat of London, the landing at Normandy, and on and on. . . ."

"You think that that's what Brown has in mind? For Barritos?"

"He ain't gonna make another Disney World out of it!"

"My God," I said, "I hope not. I'm still trying to pay off my bill from Disney World in Florida. For what it costs to go to Disney

World you could live out the rest of your days on an acre and a half at the Waldorf-Astoria and with room service. How the hell can people afford it? I mean the common people?''

"My boy," Cousin Shapiro gave me a fatherly pat on the shoulder, "There *are* no *common people—only common conceptions.*"

"What the hell does that mean?''

"I haven't the slightest idea, I am but a poor Army and Navy Store proprietor in a small town in a remote section of the Amazon valley, trying to make a living for myself and my poor bedridden wife.''

This was news. "*Bed*ridden wife?'' I said.

"Where else?'' Cousin Shapiro said. "In the back seat of a Chevy?''

"Oh,'' I said, "a Chinese joke.''

"Half and half,'' he said. "Now, let's get back to the Nazi. . . .''

"Look,'' I said, squirming around in my new sneakers, to make sure they were comfortable. "I don't think Brown, or Braun, is a Nazi at all. I just think—although he may be German, and very mysterious—I just think he's a little crazy—and to have something to do so he won't get more crazy, he's picked an odd hobby. He's organized a little play army.''

"With automatic rifles?''

"They may be made of wood. How do we know? I used to travel around with the Bob Hope show to army camps, before World War II, and they were all drilling with wooden guns.''

"America wasn't prepared,'' Cousin Shapiro said, quickly, and lighted what looked very much like a pipe for opium.

"Mind if I smoke?'' he said.

Cousin Shapiro was right about America not being prepared before we got clobbered at Pearl Harbor. If the Japanese had had a better spy system they would have known that they could have walked right down Hollywood Boulevard after Pearl Harbor and nobody would have stopped them—unless, of course, Otto Preminger was shooting a street scene at Hollywood and Vine.

"Look,'' I said, "here's the money for the sneakers and thank you, I'm going back to the plantation. Reiko and the kids want to go swimming and so do I—and you'd better forget about Mr. Brown-Braun—he's just a kook."

"Yeah," Cousin Shapiro said, "that's what they used to say about Hitler—and Charlie Manson—and Gore Vidal."

15

The longer Dr. Ramsey stayed in Barritos, the more Reiko and I felt we should help her with what was left of her five hundred cases of condoms. That is, put them to the good use for which they were intended. One trip into downtown Barritos could convince even the most hardened non-Malthusianist to soften considerably if he were anywhere near human.

The sight and sound of poverty was everywhere. Tiny children clinging to your trouser legs, begging, "Por favor, Por favor. Please. Please—" Their eyes were big with hunger. They didn't beg with the rock-hard insistence of the professional beggar. They pleaded, for life.

We always had a large supply of small coins but because there were so many children we really couldn't have carried enough for all. We gave them what we had and quickly ducked into a clothing store, or the post office, or whatever—but never into a restaurant or café. That would have been too much for them, and us. I guess we were stupidly making believe that food didn't exist.

I must confess that our hope for Dr. Ramsey's success was not entirely motivated by compassion. In back of our tiny little avaricious minds we hoped that if Dr. Ramsey could get rid of her rubbers we could sell our rubber. Our warehouses were dangerously bulging. I warned everyone not to walk too close to the walls. I thought that at any moment we might all be bounced to death by thousands of fifty-pound rubber balls.

Hurd Cambridge, of course, with his millions of acres of Brazil nuts was against any kind of birth control.

"I need bodies!" he said.

"We know that," I said, "you say it often enough." Hurd bristled at this.

"What the hell do you know, you Yankee bastard," was his gracious reply.

"A lot more than you think, you English bastard," I replied, equally as gracious. "What good are millions of tons of nuts if there's nobody around to eat them, and another thing, even here in this awesomely large country, there'll come a day when there won't be any room for you to grow your goddamn nuts. Unless you plant trees in people's heads."

"That's an idea," Hurd agreed, pleasantly, and downed another straight Gilbey's. "An idea—and it might break the monotony of this goddamn god-forsaken jungle—"

"You break the monotony enough screwing every little native broad who gets anywhere within grabbing distance of those clammy hands of yours," Elizabeth, Hurd's wife, threw in, lightly.

"How about you, dear. You're nothing but a hooker who happened to be born a lady. . . ."

"How sweet," Elizabeth said, dumping her martini into Hurd's lap, "and a very entrancing combination. A lady and a hooker—sounds like fun."

"You ought to know," Hurd said, "you and the Pete El Jaguar. I've never seen you two together without your hand up his fly so fast. How do you do it?"

"Easy," Elizabeth said. "He doesn't button it."

"Is he really a bandit?" Reiko wanted to know.

"I don't think he's a bandit in the true sense," Hurd said. "He undoubtedly rips off a tourist once in awhile, or sends his 'gang' out to roll a few drunks on a Saturday night, which is the best night for that, but I don't think he ever stuck up a railroad train or knocked off a bank or anything that would take effort. He's too goddamn busy talking about it to do it."

"I don't know," Elizabeth Cambridge said, pseudo-mysteriously, like she *did* know. "I just hope your payroll gets here tomorrow from Manaus." Hurd was instantly alert, "What do you know about any payroll coming from Manaus tomorrow? I didn't say anything about it."

"I know," Elizabeth said, sweetly irritating, "Pete told me about it."

"Hurd was on his feet, "I'd better call Pancho."

"Who's Pancho?" Reiko asked.

"He's the chief of police, Barritos," Hurd said.

"He *knows* about it."

"What?"

"The payroll from Manaus—Pancho knows about it—he's helping Pete."

"Pete and Pancho?"

"Sounds like the Sunshine Boys," Reiko said, which was pretty funny considering she had no idea what she said.

Hurd left the room, "I'm going to call Brasília," he said.

"That ought to be interesting," Elizabeth said. "I hope the janitor hears the phone."

Reiko and I, Hurd and Elizabeth had been sitting in the patio of the Barritos Yacht Club, having a few long cool drinks and trying to get our body temperatures down below 120 degrees in the shade, which was uphill all the way in Barritos where the sidewalks were hot enough to fry eggs on, and had led to a city ordinance and signs all over the place: "Curb Your Eggs"—to which no one paid the slightest attention.

Why Barritos had a yacht club was a very moot question, because outside of the *Lola Falana,* which used to be called the *Diana Ross,* and until that the *Dionne Warwicke,* and before that the *Bella Abzug,* before the owner heard her shouting once on his ultra-hi-frequency radio, Barritos had nothing which could be called a yacht, either in size or shape. The riverboats were punts and carried native fruits and vegetables from the back country to the Barritos marketplace. Still there wasn't a wino or an alcoholic in Barritos who didn't think that a yacht club wasn't a great idea.

The owner of the Barritos Yacht Club, Ricco Luciano, Jr., was a former off-duty cop from New York. I call him an off-duty cop, because that's the way it always seems to be in the *Daily News.*

* * *

OFF-DUTY COP CAPTURES BANDIT!

OFF-DUTY COP KILLS BAR PATRON!

BAR PATRON KILLS OFF-DUTY COP!

and

OFF-DUTY COP KILLS OFF-DUTY POLICE OFFICER!

All the action in New York seems to involve only off-duty cops. There may be other kinds of cops, but the *Daily News* never mentions them.

I think Ricco Luciano, Jr., was also an off-duty gangster. He talked out of the side of his mouth like he was having a tea in the Big House with George Raft, Edward G. Robinson, and Charlie Bronson. In fact, he looked like Charlie Bronson, and he was always putting calls to Vegas, Atlantic City, and some candy store in Bloomington, Illinois. Ricco Luciano, Jr., made me nervous. When he sat down with us I always worried that the Purple Gang from Detroit would suddenly slam in through the door, fire a burst from a Thompson machine gun at Junior, and hit me. It never happened, of course, but every time Ricco sat down with us and bought a round of drinks, I excused myself for a trip to the little boy's room (in which there were never any little boys).

Today was different—I was either bold or sloshed—I never did find out, but I said to Ricco, in a particularly nasty tone, "Ricco Luciano—" I was looking at him with a sort of smirky smile that anywhere in the world can get your face punched out. "Ricco," I said, "what the hell is your *real* name?"

"Merwyn Bogue," he said.

I didn't know it was going to be that easy.

"I used to be known as Ish Kabbible. I used to sing with Kay Kyser's band—remember Kay Kyser and his Kollege of Musical Knowledge? He was very big in radio."

Now, I didn't know what to believe. Had Ricco Luciano suddenly developed an incipient sense of humor or was he telling the truth? I guess I'll never know because just at that moment Hurd came back to the table and announced that everything had been arranged. For seventeen cruzeiros (three dollars in U.S.) Pancho the Barritos police chief and Pete the bandit (?) were going to guard the payroll from Manaus. Guard it against *what* was never established. Maybe Munchkins. Anyway, tomorrow would be a crimeless day in Barritos.

Hurd was glad to see Merwyn (née Ricco) sitting at the table and gave him a Brazilian hug, which was very much like the Italian hug (between men) with one exception. Brazilians kiss each other's noses, which gives the whole performance the appearance of a New Guinea blowfish mating dance.

"Ricco," Hurd wasted no time. "How about the rest of these crates of condoms, stacked up on the dock. What are we gonna do about them?"

"Well," Ricco appeared to be thinking (a feat of which I'm sure he had never been capable). "How about dumping them into the harbor—you know like during the Revolution—like the Newark Tea Party."

"Wasn't that," I foolishly interceded, "the *Boston* Tea Party?"

"They had one *there*, too?" Ricco said. I shut up henceforth.

"We can't do any rough stuff," Hurd said.

"No, I guess not," Ricco said. "Not to a broad with them kinda boobs. It'd be be a—a—"

"Sacrilege?" Elizabeth said.

"What's that?" Ricco wanted to know. So did Reiko.

"It's like desecrating something sacred," Hurd explained.

"Oh," Ricco said.

"Oh," Reiko said.

"Wait a minute," I said. "Don't you understand what Dr. Ramsey is trying to do—and leave her cantilevered construction out of it—for the moment. She is trying to save this little section of the world against itself. She is doing us all a big favor."

"Not for me, she isn't," Hurd Cambridge complained. "The population dies out who the hell is gonna pick my nuts? Elizabeth and I?"

"Include me out on that," Elizabeth said, and laughed merrily.

"There won't be any nuts to pick," I said, a little louder than I meant to. "They'll be trampled under by a mass of people. Listen, it took millions of years to populate this earth by a billion people—that was in 1850—there were one billion people on earth by the year 1850. Eighty years later in 1930 there were two billion human beings on earth, thirty years later in 1960 there were three billion, and on March 28th, 1976, on a Sunday night, the *four billionth* person was *born!*"

"It was a boy and he was Chinese!" Cousin Shapiro said, and he pulled up a chair, directly in front of Hurd Cambridge.

"Well," Hurd said. "It's the Jewish Chink. I didn't know they allowed shopkeepers in here."

"Only on the Queen's birthday," Cousin Shapiro answered. If this annoyed Hurd, he didn't react.

"We were just talking about Dr. Ramsey and—"

"Sounds like fun," Cousin Shapiro said, "I haven't seen them around lately."

"They're around," Elizabeth Cambridge said. "Around and bouncing."

"Elizabeth's jealous because she can't compete in that department," Hurd said.

"Who could," Elizabeth said, "compete with the Himalayas?"

"I couldn't compete with the Berkshires," Reiko said, as usual all honesty. Of course, it was true. Japanese girls are only busty under the influence of silicone.

16

If you have ever felt yourself leaning toward experimenting with masochism, buy your seven-year-old child a drum, or better still buy him a trumpet.

And at the same time encourage your oldest boy, age fifteen, to take a few piano lessons. Then as a topper and a pièce de résistance on the Royal Road to Raving Maniacville, sit before your television set watching the six-o'clock news while they both practice at the same time—three feet away. It will be an unforgettable experience—if you are ever to remember anything again.

We found that there really wasn't much for Bobby and Timothy to do in and around Barritos. There were a few children they could play with near our rubber ranch, but they spoke only Portuguese or some brand of Indian language, which didn't seem to be too well understood, even by the ones who spoke Portuguese. But as you all know, language is no barrier among children. That comes later, with age and wisdom—at the U.N.

At first the sheer novelty of playing with real Indians provided our kids with one of the big moments of their lives, one they'll remember always. But like all novelties, as Alexander King used to say, even sex with a double-jointed bearded lady palls after the third or fourth time. (Maybe you didn't say that, Alex, wherever you are, but I like to think you might have.)

Bobby and Timothy got tired of playing cowboys and Indians where the Indians always won. (And why not? They had blow-guns against my kids' poison Frisbies.) The other native kids, the ones who only spoke Portuguese, would play nothing but *futebol* (soccer). Each kid wanted to be Pelé, the greatest *futebol* player of them all and a greater hero in Brazil than George Washington or Catfish Hunter is in his native country. Bobby and Timothy played *futebol* day and night for the first three months we were settling down in Barritos. I had told them if they wanted to make friends with the other kids in the neighborhood they would have to go along and play whatever games the other kids played—and they'd have to act like they were enjoying themselves. They endured this as long as they could, then one day Bobby and Timothy introduced these innocent children of the jungle to *Kung Fu,* and in no time at all these innocent jungle children were beating the hell out of the two wise-ass Connecticut Yankees.

Reiko intervened with large bowls of vanilla ice cream smeared with hot chocolate and chopped nuts, for one and all. This stopped the war immediately and it was never resumed. Maybe this would work in Lebanon. (Something better work there—the guests in the Holiday Inn are getting mighty fed up with all the noise.)

I felt sorry for Bobby and Timothy because wherever we've lived since they were born, we've made it hard for them to find playmates. Either the other kids lived miles away, by dogsled, or something else happened, such as now. There were plenty of kids around, which had never happened to my sons before, but the kids were just one step away from being head-hunters. I may have been acting like another overly-anxious father, but these kids carried knives. The knives were supposedly for cutting up melons or something they'd trapped or shot for lunch, but I pictured little José and whoever at a tense moment in a tie *futebol* match, whipping the blades from their belts and slicing out the necessity for any extra overtime play.

The reason, I think that Bobby and Timothy grew bored with *futebol* as quickly as they did was because these tricky little Barritos boys were so good at it. Every day before a game they'd run down to the church and have the Reverend Meech bless the *futebol.* I never believed, along with Joe Namath, that blessing a *futebol* would influence the outcome of a game, but whatever—it may not have worked in the Superbowl, but it sure worked in Barritos.

Just for the hell of it, one day, I asked the Reverend Meech what he said when he blessed the *futebol*. A beatific smile wreathed his lips, and he said, "That's between me and the *futebol*, but because *you* are a true believer—in *what*, I wouldn't care to know—I'll tell you. I say to the *futebol*, "It doesn't matter if you win or lose it's how you play the game. So use your own dice."

"What?" I said, "That sounds like a lousy joke. That you made up."

"It's not that," The Reverend Meech said. "Before I became a man of the cloth I used to watch Tony Orlando and Dawn."

I couldn't believe it but I said, "Reverend Meech, that brings up a question—maybe you can answer it—*why* is there a *Tony Orlando* and *Dawn*?"

"Because," the Reverend Meech said, "God can't be everywhere."

The music teachers, or at least the piano and trumpet teachers of Barritos were good. Very good. Although I believed at first that they were self-taught, this was not the case. "Fat Lips" Gonzales (as he was called) had attended the conservatory in São Paulo for six years and was practically a virtuoso on the trumpet. Why he had left the fun, frolic, and good pay of São Paulo was a question we felt we shouldn't ask, but we did and it seems that he left that crowded metropolis, far to the south of Barritos, a few minutes before the police broke down the door to his cozy little apartment. They wanted to ask him questions about a fellow brass-section member who was found behind the bandstand at the São Paulo Palais de Dance with the first four notes of Beethoven's Fifth Symphony expertly and neatly carved into his forehead by something sharp. "Fat Lips" explained: "This guy—I don' like him. He play flat. He play sharp. He don' play in between."

"You killed him?" Reiko was shocked.

"No, but he's life is now miserable. Everywhere he go, he has to try and explain his forehead." Then he added, "Very difficult to do—in Portuguese."

"Fat Lips" was teaching Timothy the trumpet, and Timothy was learning at an astonishing rate. So far, he hasn't returned home from a lesson with any messages on his forehead. A good sign.

Bobby also surprised us, first by his interest in the piano, and then by his remarkable strides in learning. We never have to urge him to practice. Mostly we have to urge him not to. He's too goddamn avid.

Our first problem was obtaining a piano. It took us all of three months. The Captain of the *Lola Falana* refused to haul one up from Belém, because he hated music. Later we found out why. In his youth he had picked up a little something from Chiquita Mocha, who had been the piano player in the Café Gloria B.P. (before penicillin).

Someone suggested we check the old Barritos opera house, which had been built during the rubber boom by the rubber rich plantation owners, and at various times in its short history had featured all the opera greats of the day, from Galli-Curci, Caruso up and down. They had all sung there and were paid off in gold (and rubber balls).

The reasoning that prompted the suggestion that we look around the basement of the old opera house was logical—they must have used a piano. Caruso would not have sung accompanied by a banjo and a frisco whistle.

The basement of the old opera house, which after much red tape and flack from the local D.A.R. (Daughters of the Amazon Rubber Rooters) we obtained permission to explore, was just a little smaller than the Carlsbad Caverns and just as full of bats, and I may be wrong but I thought I saw a few skeletons (non-union stagehands?).

The dust in the Old Barritos Opera House was at least a foot deep at the level we were exploring. At first we found nothing in the way of musical instruments, except a few old balalaikas (formerly owned by some musical defectors from the land of the Czar back in the days when the Russians didn't know that they had it so good). We also found a smashed ukulele with the initials A.G. spelled out in rhinestones (Arthur Godfrey?) (Antoine Guggenheim?) (Argyle Götterdämmerung?)

Along about the third day we were growing discouraged. Reiko was ready to give up and so was I, but Bobby persisted—he wanted a piano. We had spent so much time in the catacombs, as we called them, I was getting anxious about our rubber trees. I wondered if the boys who were supposed to empty the latex buckets every other day were doing it, or if we would get back to the plantation and find it stickily inundated. I could just picture us in our driveway, awash in our old Volkswagen, sending up flares and signals to the Coast Guard, "Mayday! Mayday! Help! we are foundering in twenty-six fathoms of Elmer's Glue!"

I could also imagine the Coast Guard ignoring this weirdo cry for assistance. And writing it off as some UFO message from a bunch of Martians high on grass (Mars Gold).

Bobby was the one who finally found a piano, but not in the basement crypt. The piano was upstairs on the stage and there wasn't a speck of dust on it. Just a few cobwebs and a note written on a sheet of manuscript on the music stand. It read: "Whoever finds this piano—I love you. Signed A. Rubenstein, July 17, 1903. P.S. It needs tuning."

There was a lot more red tape in obtaining the piano for Bobby. Money was no problem. They *gave* us the piano. Of course the intervention by Hurd Cambridge, the Reverend Meech, Pancho Bocachica, the Barritos police chief, and Pete El Jaguar helped immensely. They all threatened the mayor, Señor Casseres—who dressed like Adolphe Menjou—one at a time and collectively until he finally gave in and allowed us to borrow it for twenty years. I think it was the Reverend Meech who persuaded him, by threatening to bar him from the church and bury him (when he died) in unconsecrated ground. This unnerved the mayor until he suddenly realized, after it was too late, that he was Catholic and the Reverend Meech was a Protestant and had no clout whatsoever with Pope Paul. Add to that the fact that when the Reverend Meech was loaded, which was more than occasionally, he kept confusing Pope Paul with Peter and Mary and their singing together at Caesar's Palace (which he thought was still in Rome).

After Bobby had his piano and Timothy had his trumpet and they both were taking lessons, from that day on we were entertained as we have never been entertained before—anywhere—Wolves howling in chorus near our Canadian bush home, coyotes at midnight in California, snowmobiles through our living room at three in the morning in Maine, and coon hunters blasting away all night in Connecticut. These last four we learned to live with, but with our own children—"omne vivum ex ovo."

17

North America tends to lump South America together as one large crazy-quilt of revolutions, held together (or apart) by mountains, rivers, and soldiers. And this time, North America is correct in its assumption. There is not one country in South America, at the moment, which is not ruled by a military junta. And ruled badly. No matter if the New York *Times'* full page ads with pictures of the beach in Rio with Jesus standing on the mountain top blessing the tourists (with money) infer that life in Rio is just one long carnival, with millions of string-bikini almost-covered girls running up and down the beach looking just for *you,* it's not quite that way. Bombs go off in cars, or department stores, or toilets and bodies are minced and scattered. Soldiers, or whatever they are, enter houses, seemingly for no reason, to bayonet men, women and children at random, then disappear back into the black void from which they came.

What's it all about? No one knows. South America is still a continent of the very rich and the very poor. I guess that's what it's all about. Somebody wants *everybody* poor—with that somebody in charge and living at the palace, naturally.

Barritos had had no problems so far. The government was light-years away, and the officials presumably sent up from Brasília had been chosen for the district of Barritos because they had absolutely no knowledge of the interior and a great inclination to know less. They adopted or were to join the Barritos Yacht Club and that was their base. I doubt if either of them know the location of their official residence or had bothered to inquire. The Yacht Club, with its excellent supply of the liquors of the world and the pretty serving bunnies—or Armadillos as they were called in Barritos—was the only office they needed to carry out their official duties, one of which was attempting to collect the tax on rubber and nuts. But as a local wit (there was only one) remarked, "Trying to collect taxes in Barritos is like trying to play scrabble in a bowl of alphabet soup. With your bare feet. With the lights out." The Barritos local wit was extremely low-powered even at his apogee. His IQ could only be gauged by a bored statistician, who was sick and tired of measuring Pygmy penises for the Smithsonian. (The Smithsonian, incidentally, has the second largest collection of Pygmy penis data in the world. Second only to Shelley Winters'.)

Some of what I write may be libelous. God, I hope so! Publicity is so important!

The government officials recently sent up, presumably from Brasília, were actually only two in number; Señor "Castanhas" (nuts) who was crazy, and Señor "Chourico" (sausage) who was fat. Together they were known by the Yacht Club's Bunnies (Armadillos) as El "Coelhos" (the rabbits).

This combination of the two representatives of Presidente Whomever's Brazilian government, and the Yacht Club's hutch of twitchy armadillos boded no good for Dr. Ramsey's program of abstinence—or at least, precaution.

Dr. Ramsey tried to explain this in her pidgin Portuguese to the Cashew and the Bratwurst, as we were now calling them, but they misinterpreted, purposely I'm sure, and by signs (mostly pornographic) and by far out (for Dr. Ramsey) Portuguese words they managed to communicate that they'd be delighted to wear her funny little red and green and blue rubber hats if that's what she needed to turn her on as they rolled around the Pampas with her. *Why* mostly everyone in Brazil kept mistaking condoms for *headgear* is mysterious. Or *is* it?

I'm sure that Dr. Ramsey would not have gone above and beyond the call of duty to demonstrate her theory, but she was rapidly reaching the point of no return in the area of patience. Veronica Ramsey was intelligent to such a degree that if she had been short dumpy-fat and pimply she would have been unbearable. But since she was blessed with a figure which went beyond divine and a face which was certainly one of the most beautiful I have ever seen—and I've looked—combined with a thick mane of golden red hair that came tumbling over her shoulders, reaching toward the most tantalizing pair of dimpled (I knew) buttocks ever to tease a man down from king to a slavering serf, she could harangue everyone with the same dull story over and over again about how she could not get the natives to cooperate and we all just listened and loved it. Every outraged gesture she made in protest against the ignorance and indifference of the people of Barritos was a movement of lithesome beauty. Fifty years ago this would have been Isadora Duncan dancing in a single veil in a field of clover in a Maxfield Parrish blue light to strains of "Clair de Lune" instead of a U.S. government doctor pleading with a bunch of bar flies in a dingy back jungle saloon to *get out there* and *teach* those *simple savages* to *wear condoms!*

Dr. Ramsey had taken to staging her Billy Graham revival meetings, as she herself now called them, at the Barritos Yacht Club, because that was where it was at—the only action for thousands of miles around was right there. The crowds grew larger as the weeks went by, and not all of the customers had come to hear Veronica Ramsey give her by now well known spiel about our earth becoming so inundated by the human race that soon we would be eating each other. This, of course, got an hysterical reaction every time Dr. Ramsey mentioned it.

Dr. Ramsey at the Barritos Yacht Club was becoming a greater attraction than Caruso and Galli-Curci together had ever been at the old Barritos Opera House.

But some of the groups were tucked away into the dark corners (of which there were plenty in the Yacht Club—due to a little generator that couldn't, most of the time). These groups talked among themselves in gutterals, and looked, to Reiko and me, like hoodlums or as they are probably called in South America—guerrillas. Che Guevara's Boy Scouts. They all carried knives that could have been called swords. They were enormous, and sharp. One night just to prove this one of this ominous gang grabbed George Burns' (who happened to be a Lindblad tourista that night) toupee and sliced it in half with one stroke—then gave half of it back to George. George quickly placed it at the front end of his forehead, passed out cigars and left.

There was always another gang, I noticed, sitting with Mr. Brown. They all sat stiff and erect like they had just graduated from Heidelberg and were in town for a beer. They never laughed or sang as the others at the Yacht Club did. They just sat there for the evening, not enjoying themselves if they could help it.

Although Cousin Shapiro was the only part-Chinese in Barritos he suddenly seemed to have a lot of relatives visiting him from Taiwan. They were a bunch of tough little monkeys and they laughed at everything, especially if nothing was funny. That's when they laughed loudest.

Pete El Jaguar and *his* vicious-looking bunch were usually among the crowd. They looked like some movie producer had put out a call for pirate types and got every one that Central Casting ever had.

The Reverend Meech never went home, it seemed. He shared a table or tables with the guru, who had a new kick (besides a lovely dyed-blonde Mato Grasso Indian girl, dressed as a nun with a slit skirt). The guru wore a turban that contained a little pot filled with burning incense. The guru was fat—very fat—and the burning incense in his hat gave him the appearance of an untested nuclear device about to explode and spoil everybody's fun.

The Reverend Meech brought along his wife, Norma-Lee, who adored him and everything he did. Even when the Reverend Meech slipped his clammy little paw inside the guru's nun's navel-cut habit and pinched her nipples, Norma-Lee screamed with laughter, and the guru burned the back of the Reverend Meech's hand with a super-charged cattle prod he always carried ("to keep his little flock in line" he said). The cattle prod would have killed the toughest Texas longhorn, but with the Reverend Meech he just got a second degree burn and it fused his gold inlays together—forever.

The Barritos chief of police was always there at the Yacht Club. No matter what happened there—a stabbing, a few pistol shots, a fist fight—he never left his place at the bar and never stopped smiling and never stopped saying "very nice, very nice" for the benefit of any American tourists who might be listening.

Mr. and Mrs. Tooze seemed to like Barritos and stayed on and on. They never missed a night at the Yacht Club, and Mrs. Tooze was probably the most popular Yankee ever to visit Brazil. Her waving of the long broom handle with the red, white and blue condom rolled onto it was now a legend, and many a native guitar player/composer had killed everybody softly with his newly composed song about this wondrous and massive sight.

One night, I could have sworn, Fidel Castro showed up—unless somebody was playing a joke. Nobody noticed but us, and Dr. Ramsey and Mr. and Mrs. Tooze. It must have been Castro; he was surrounded by at least thirty or forty Cuban soldiers carrying automatic rifles, at the ready.

It must have been Castro because he never stopped talking. He never stopped smoking either and pretty soon everybody in the place was turning blue.

Mrs. Tooze got up and walked over to Castro and asked him very nicely if he'd mind putting out his goddamned cigar before he killed every living thing in Barritos. Castro smiled and stubbed out his big fat Cuban cigar, and we all started breathing again.

When Mrs. Tooze (whom I have to admire for stupidity and guts) showed us an autograph she'd gotten from him, it read, "To the Gutsy Mrs. Tooze—with admiration—signed Mickey Rooney." It had to be Castro.

18

One day, the climate of Barritos changed. The political climate. I think it was the day the Angolan troops arrived. A small group but they had machine pistols, mortars, .50 caliber machine guns, hand grenades, human tooth necklaces and sidearms. From that day every citizen of Barritos, as if by some sort of secret agreement started carrying pistols. On their hips—in shoulder holsters, ankle holsters, crotch holsters, and no holsters. They just toted them around in their hands.

I dropped by the Yacht Club to ask Cashew and Bratwurst, the two government officials from Brasília, what the hell? They just giggled. I don't know whether they understood that as a resident and taxpayer (?) of Barritos I had a right to know what a bunch of gun-loaded Angolan soldiers were doing in our town, and also why the hell every private citizen was armed to the teeth, and where could I buy a Colt .45 and three .22 pistols for Reiko, Bobby, and Timothy? They giggled a lot more after this and so did all of the big-bosomed armadillos who were bending over them at the time, serving them their triple planters punches, which now came in a 50-ounce glass that necessitated that you had to stand on your chair to drink it.

Bratwurst paid one of the armadillos in silver cruzeiros, and he dropped them in the deep valley between her breasts—I listened and it took almost three seconds before I heard the clink as they hit bottom.

We learned nothing from the government jokers, as we knew we wouldn't. Cousin Shapiro's Army and Navy store was only a few blocks down Main Street (or as it was known as in Barritos: Avenida Del Los Pizzaro Y Cortez Y Western Auto). We had to find out if the danger was real or it was just the good old South American custom of the bloodless coup where only fifty or sixty people got shot dead. Cousin Shapiro interrupted his solitaire Mah-Jong game to fill us in on conditions, as he saw them. The black soldiers were not Angolans at all, he said. They were the remnants of Duke Ellington's band who had had enough of rock in Harlem and decided to move south. The guns and all the other armaments were just for protection—in case they were jumped by deserters from Lawrence Welk who, it was reputed, had been hiding for years in the Brazilian jungles. An apocryphal bit of information, but if Cousin Shapiro got pleasure out of repeating it I for one would not deny him. We could see that Cousin Shapiro was not going to give us any information, but he did sell us guns, because, he explained, "You never can tell when you'll bump into a tiger or elephant some night on the highway—and they can be mean!" I accepted this, and bought the three .22 pistols for Reiko, Bobby and Timothy. (Timothy's I didn't load.) Reiko was scared of pistols "because they were always accidentally going off and killing somebody." I explained to her that no pistol ever went off "accidentally"—somebody has to pull the trigger, and to pull the trigger on a pistol, that hasn't been rigged, takes quite a pull.

"What about Andy Williams' wife?" Reiko said, "That was an accident?"

"Of course," I agreed, "And that's why they call them Saturday Night Specials."

"What's a Saturday Night Special?" Reiko asked.

"A bottle of booze," Bobby said. The kid had something there.

We felt like the Dalton gang, walking down the street after being armed at Cousin Shapiro's. But there was no reason to feel self-conscious, because we certainly were not alone in our display of preparedness—preparedness for *what* we still didn't know. I had the feeling that the fascination of being a big South American rubber planter was draining away rapidly.

In front of the Yacht Club we met Mr. and Mrs. Tooze. Mr. Tooze was unarmed, but Mrs. Tooze was carrying a loaded water pistol. And a plastic dagger.

"I don't want to get raped," she explained—wistfully.

Hurd Cambridge and the lovely Elizabeth were waiting for us when we got back to Casa Las Bombas. They waved a tentative greeting as they sat sprawled in our chaise longues under the somewhat coolness of our palm-treed patio. They both had drinks and were quite relaxed, and soon Reiko and I relaxed with them, while Bobby and Timothy went off to play *futebol* with their little machete-equipped friends in the searing heat of the brilliant Amazonas day.

"Been buying guns?" Hurd asked, none too brightly, I felt.

"No," I said, indicating my Government Model Colt .45 automatic. "This is made out of chocolate. I'm saving it for Easter. Then I'm going to eat it all at once and get sick."

"That's what I like about you Douglas," Hurd said, "You are absolutely fearless. You can laugh right in the face of death—you're also a little stupid."

"You're right," I agreed, "I could have stayed back in Connecticut and had nothing to worry about except going to the bakery to order a birthday cake and wind up getting shot to death in the backroom along with five other people. Did you read about that?"

He hadn't and he didn't care.

"Jack," Hurd said, pinching his beautiful Elizabeth's enticing behind which was conveniently hanging out the back of the director's chair she was now sitting in, "Something's afoot."

"We know," Reiko said, "but nobody'll tell us anything and we can't speak enough of the language to find out."

"Even then you wouldn't find out," Elizabeth said and sucked in a long draught of her Tom Collins.

"I don't think anyone knows," Hurd said. "Even if there was another revolution or uprising or coup or whatever the hell they're calling them now, I don't think it would affect us up here. We're too goddamn far away from everything—and God knows there's no money up here that they can grab. Not that they know of anyway," he added enigmatically, "and that's all they're interested in."

"Have you heard about Nelson Rockefeller coming down here?" Elizabeth asked.

"Nelson Rockefeller!" You're kidding!" I was astonished.

"Who would kid about Nelson Rockefeller?" Hurd asked, with a touch of controlled patience.

"He's coming down to visit 'Doctor' Veronica Ramsey," Elizabeth said, archly. Very archly.

"Oh, come on," I said, "Nelson doesn't fool around. He's beyond all that."

"I heard he uses Preparation H to hold up the bags under his eyes," Elizabeth said.

This stopped me for a moment because I had heard that some people were using the hemorrhoid helper to tighten their eyes, but I had never heard of this in connection with the former Vice-President. "That's a goddamn lie!" was my brilliant retort.

Elizabeth sucked up half of her Tom Collins before she replied, "Jack Baby," she said. "Don't get so upset, I'm not attacking any sacred American institutions or anything like that. I'm just talking about a man who uses Preparation H in a peculiar way—so relax."

"Look," I said, "I don't care if he shoves it up his ass . . .!"

Elizabeth screamed with laughter, and I'll admit I had to join her.

"When's he going to be here in Barritos?" I said.

"Soon, that's all I know," Hurd said.

"He's going to stay with us," Elizabeth said. "We got the notice from the State Department yesterday, but they didn't say when. They just said 'Get the Presidential Suite ready!!!!' "

"The Presidential Suite," I said, "You got a Presidential Suite?"

"We have now," Hurd said. "We bought purple sheets and we have a gold vulture over the door."

"A gold—*vulture*—over the door?" I said.

"Yeah," Hurd said. "It was the closest thing Cousin Shapiro had to an eagle."

19

At last—it happened! A buyer for our rubber! This was almost a miracle. At almost exactly the moment when our warehouses could not possibly have held another fifty-pound ball of unprocessed rubber, the El Exigente of the rubber business came along. He saw our rubber. He pinched our rubber. He cut open our rubber. He liked our rubber and he bought our rubber.

This rubber buyer looked exactly like Rasputin, and he had a thick accent. I'm sure it was Russian, but we didn't care. Their rubles were as good as anybody's.

He had come up the river in his own boat. A huge craft, capable of carrying many tons of any kind of cargo, it was a boat built especially for a river like the Amazon, whose channel changed almost from day to day, so that Amazon pilots have to be very cagey about which sand bar they can cross and which they can't. But this stranger's boat was equipped with the very latest of sounding gear for sonar navigation and it had made it up the river from Belém with no difficulty whatsoever.

The one-hundred-and-three-year-old man, who owned the Barritos town dock and also the good ship *Lola Falana,* was rather put out by the use of this new vessel to carry our rubber. We tried to explain, but out Portuguese never got through to him and he spent all of his time while the new ship was getting loaded, doing the same thing at the Yacht Club. Our sympathies were with him, but our bank account looked a lot better after Rasputin's check had cleared and he had sailed.

We've never found out who this mysterious stranger was, but we're eternally grateful to him for his purchase, and I hope whatever rubber product he made from our latex balls turned out to be a great success in the commercial world. Even if he had made rubber tracks for Soviet tanks so they could sneak up behind China and scare hell out of her. I think China needs a good scare besides Nixon.

The sale of our rubber led to plans for a big celebration party at Casa Las Bombas. We felt we owed it to ourselves.

The guest list for our grand bash read like the who's who of Barritos, and what else could it have been? It would not have made sense to invite Mr. and Mrs. Gene Saks, and Mr. and Mrs. Larry Gelbart, and Mr. and Mrs. Hal Kanter, and Mr. and Mrs. Grant Tinker of Santa Monica, Bel Air, Brentwood, Beverly Hills, and Malibu, to an evening's get-together in Barritos, Brazil. Not that they wouldn't all have come, but at the end of the evening, after those long good-byes and that long ride home, none of them would have ever spoken to us again.

Dr. Ramsey was first on our list (she had always been first on my list) then came, not necessarily in order of their importance or alphabetically: Hurd and Elizabeth Cambridge, who could be counted on for a good four-letter-word screaming fight; Pete El Jaguar, the self-styled Robinhood bandit, whose hard-on for Elizabeth would be the cause of the four-letter-word fight, the Reverend Meech, accompanied by the dyed-blond Mato Grasso Indian nun, with one or two breasts hanging out, and his wife Norma-Lee, who approved the thought that the benevolent Reverend Meech was rubbing holy water onto the dyed blond nun's nipples to keep them safe from harm, Cousin Shapiro, who would show up either dressed like Ghengis or Sammy Kahn, Mr. Brown the suspected Nazi, whose Teutonic charm shone through his Storm Trooper shyness like a mugger's blackjack. The guru Mahareshi Nepal with his smokey turban, his crystal ball, and his platoon of concubine-groupies who would have their fortunes and their Mount of Venus read at the same time, Mr. and Mrs. Tooze, who somehow had become part of the local scene and when it came to parties they were always good for a groan and a temperance lecture from Mrs. Tooze—usually delivered from underneath a table. The local witch doctor whom we now called Herbie Turtletaub, because it sounded better than his real name, which we had given up trying to pronounce. He was invited because it was the only way we could keep an eye on him because of his hobby of throwing the local virgins into the local volcano. We also invited the hundred-and-three-year-old man who owned the dock and the *Lola Falana*—we were hoping he'd do the limbo then we'd never have to invite him again. There was Señor Cassares, the Barritos mayor, who dressed like Adolphe Menjou. We invited him because he always fell asleep and Mogo, the chief of the pygmies always danced on him trying to wake him up, which meant of course, we had to invite Mogo who was a lot of fun at parties and who always won the limbo contest without even bending over. We invited the Barritos police chief who's "very nice, very nice" provided background music to Mrs. Tooze's late evening screaming "Fuck me! Fuck me! Fuck Me!" to anyone who would listen. She even yelled it to the wooden tiki we had brought years ago from Tahiti. The tiki was mostly a large wooden schlong and it did something to Mrs. Tooze—although it couldn't do anything to Mrs. Tooze.

We invited Pierre Leuthold, who was trying to write a sexy book about the mating habits of the South American savages and getting nowhere with his writing because his research was so time consuming (he didn't even miss his typewriter when it was stolen).

We invited Irv Vesco, the financier-embezzler-crook-tycoon who happened to be in town, on his way to a new secret hiding place which was about as secret as Quaker Oats.

Last, and least we invited Cashew and Bratwurst, mainly because we didn't think they'd ever tear themselves away from the armadillos at the Yacht Club. (Just in passing, three of the armadillos were pregnant, and both Cashew and Bratwurst were taking credit and they were probably both right.)

The night of our big party to celebrate our rubber sale followed a day of almost perfect weather for that region of the upper Amazon River. There was no humidity—which happens rarely. The air was cool and refreshing—also rare—and the sky was of the deepest blue of the deepest ocean. We were ecstatic, remembering other outdoor parties, especially in California, which had been wiped out by the weather.

At exactly six P.M. our first guest arrived. It was Mogo, chief of the pygmies. He didn't want to miss anything, and with his size he never did. He was up under every female's gown before the evenings were half over. He got slapped black and blue, which was hard to tell because he was mostly black anyway and the blue just blended right in.

As Margarita, our maid, was taking Chief Mogo's monkey-skin royal robe and his baseball-bat scepter, there was a tremendous crash of thunder and a flash of light like the hydrogen bomb. At the count of three we were in the epicenter of a cloud-burst.

The rain was the most frightening experience I have ever been through. It actually wasn't rain at all. It was a sheet of water pouring on our patio like we had suddenly been transported to a spot right under the heaviest drop of Niagara Falls, or the midst of the Snake River Canyon's most turbulent strip. We all stood there transfixed. Timothy suddenly let out a shriek as the swimming pool burst out over its concrete coping and flowed toward us like a tidal wave, albeit a minor one, but a tidal wave all the same. We dashed for the house and tried to slam doors against this towering (it seemed) wall of the wettest and quickest water I have ever seen. The doors were as nothing. The living room was immediately under at least a foot of water. Stools and cushions were flung around the room as in a giant whirlpool.

Bottles of expensive French wine were crashing into each other and sinking. The windows, which had been open, were now battering themselves to pieces in the violent winds. Pictures were torn off the walls. Glass was flying and we were praying. Even Mogo. He was saying the Lord's Prayer. Up to that moment I didn't know he could speak English. Maybe he couldn't—before.

The party was ended before it began. Five minutes later it was all over. That five minutes had seemed like a double eternity. We could not believe the scene of devastation. The water receded almost as quickly as it had come, but the floor was now wall to wall hors d'oeuvres interspersed with large and small islands of broken bottles, glasses, picture frames, vases, books, magazines, mirrors, couch cushions, couches, tiger skins, record albums, curtains, window frames, glass, glass and more glass, plus a large fifty-pound ball of crude rubber with a tiny man and woman (Reiko and me) stuck on the top of it like wedding cake dolls to celebrate our good luck. The money we had received from our rubber sale, I wondered—would it be enough to cover the damage we had just been handed as part of our celebration?

Mogo was the only party guest we saw that night and in a few minutes he took off. Without even a pygmy thank you. On his way out he grabbed an unbroken quart of Dom Pérignon '63. We got a postcard from him, later, it read:

"God bless us every one—Tiny Tim."

20

It took us—Reiko, Bobby, Timothy, four Indian handy (?) men and me—weeks to clean up the mess distributed by the flash flood and semi-tornado. Every bit of wall to wall carpeting had to be washed and dyed. It was either that or take fifteen minutes to cross the living room, it was that adhesive. We never should have mixed Twinkies with the hors d'oeuvres. Caviar is but once but Twinkies are forever, I kept thinking as I tried to scrape the acrylon back to its former condition. We finally had to give up and hire the local carpet man, who happened to be a former headhunter who did carpets as a side line. And a tax shelter. Headhunting was *not* a tax shelter.

We were just about ready to give our promised celebration party, mainly because the disappointed guests acted like we had started the catastrophic wind and water episode to get out of giving the party.

Again the invitations were sent out. And again the party was called off, not by the weather this time, but by the newly organized latex and nut workers union, which had been organized by a black man who was new in town. No sooner had he gotten everyone connected with the rubber and nut business to join together for strength—than—just to show his power, I imagine—he called a strike.

A strike among latex tappers could be ruinous. The latex buckets on the trees had to be emptied every other day, or else we would be stuck on our plantation—literally.

Something had to be done and I had to do it.

Black is beautiful. If it's Diahann Carrol or Lena Horne or Tina Turner or Harry Belafonte. If it's Godfrey Cambridge or Sammy Davis or Joe Frazier or Mohammed Maraka—the rubber and nut union organizer—forget it. Mohammed was ugly and he enjoyed it. He wore an Afro that could have nested a colony of Grackles. He could have shaded half of Watts.

"I never met a white man I didn't hate," were his first words to me when I met him at the Barritos Hilton.

"I don't blame you, I'm passing," I said, trying to keep things nice and friendly. "Are you Mohammed Maraka?"

"Don't I look like it," he said, giving me the coy pose of a female gorilla in heat. "Maybe you remember me as George Washington Carver Johnson? That was before I Algerianized it."

"I remember, now," I said. "I read about you in *Time* and *Newsweek*."

"And *Screw*," he said.

"What?" I said.

"*Screw*," he said.

"You mean, you don't want to talk? You want me to leave?" I said.

"*Screw*. It's a magazine put out by some Jewish kid. It's great, tells you everything!"

"Oh," I said, although I have been aware of *Screw* since my first copy arrived five years ago.

"You are the direct descendant of Kenyatta Muu-Muu who was sold as a slave to George Washington by the original Mohammed Maraka. Right?"

"Right on," Mohammed Maraka said, "You're smart for a honky."

"So are you," I said. "The Arabs sold all you blacks to the white man and you revere their memory by taking their Arabic names. Any significance in that?"

"Ah don't know 'bout that—" he retrogressed back into his Harlem street talk pattern and forgot about his Oxford accent. "I just think that an Arabic name sounds a little better than 'Bojangles' and them kinda names. They don't have no tone."

"No, they don't," I agreed. "Mr. Maraka, you used to be a poet and a playwright and a great friend of Angela Davis. What happened to all that?"

"It's still around," Maraka said. "Still around—"

"The last time I heard of you, up in New York, you were getting yourself arrested for leading a riot, trying to stop the white folks from building a pool hall in a black neighborhood."

"Right on." He was back into his Oxford accent now, full steam, "We felt that a white pool hall in that particular black neighborhood would lower real estate values and bring in a bad element. Like the police."

The next time I saw Mohammed Maraka—it was by "appointment only" in the Royal Suite at the Barritos Hilton (a hotel which had no connection whatever with any other Hilton in this world or the next). Mohammed Maraka was in the bathroom of the Barritos Hilton Royal Suite, which had been re-done in leopard skins instead of cherubs, and Mohammed Maraka was lolling in a perfumed milk bath and playing a stereo about fourteen times as loud as it was possible to play (according to RCA). I had to shout to make myself not heard.

I was not in Mohammed Maraka's bathroom by choice—I had been ushered in there by a black dwarf, who seemed to be part of Mohammed's entourage, and who carried a switchblade.

Mohammed lolled more than moreso in his soothingly warm milk bath, the black dwarf adding a quart of Sardo now and then. At a signal from this King of Kings, the black dwarf shut off the screaming music, and Mohammed said, "The whites are trying to take over this country from the soul-brothers."

"The whites were here first," I said, like a kindly old zoo keeper to a sick python.

"The Indians were here first!" Mohammed Maraka shouted. I thought he was about to jump from the tub and thrash me with his pine-scented sponge, but instead he suddenly subsided and the black dwarf added another quart of Sardo to his bath with just a dash of vermouth.

"Keeps my skin like velvet," Mohammed Maraka said, "Doesn't it, Irving?" The black dwarf nodded.

"The Indians," I said, "are really Chinese. Did you know that?"

Mohammed Maraka perked up.

"It's true," I continued, not knowing where or what I was up to. "The Chinese just happened to wander some nineteen thousand or so miles from their homeland by a slight navigational mistake. But they, actually, were not the first. . . ."

Maraka was staring at me, his eyes slitted shrewdly, "Who was?"

"The cave men, the bison and the dire wolves."

Mohammed Maraka relaxed markedly and said, "To me—most wolves are dire."

"That's because you don't know a goddamn thing about wolves," I said with some heat.

"Irving," Mohammed said to the black dwarf, "Stab Mr. Douglas."

"I'm sorry," I said. "I forgot why I came here."

"Never mind, Irving," Mohammed said, then turned his full attention to admiring his light chocolate hands with their vanilla palms and their orange fingernails, "Roses are red," he said, "violets are blue, sugar is sweet, and I'm a poet, you know."

"I know," I said. "Sugar is sweet and *what?*"

"I don't really know," Mohammed said, "I just can't seem to come up with a really satisfactory last line and god knows I've tried. It's a real ball-breaker," he added. Then he sighed heavily. "I never should have become a poet. I should have been a sculptor."

"That's a real ball-breaker, too," I said. "You have to lift all those heavy chunks of marble. A couple of years of that and you'd be all hernia."

"What you come here for, whitey?" Mohammed Maraka unexpectedly demanded. The air was suddenly charged, and the little black dwarf was at the ready with his switch knife.

"Oh," I said, "about this strike—?"

"You got pickets, plenty of pickets? They got signs?"

"Oh yes. We've got pickets all right and plenty of signs. It's just that, what do you want? What do they want?"

"Decent working conditions. Better housing. Pensions. Hospital insurance. Life insurance. Cost of living rise. Better cars—"

"Better cars?" I was astounded.

"Yes."

"But they don't have *any* cars now!"

"See what I mean????"

"But we don't have any roads. Where are they gonna drive?"

Mohammed Maraka thought for a moment, then he suddenly screamed, "Better roads!!!!!!!!"

21

The rubber strike continued. Things were getting very gummy around Casa Las Bombas. Roosters were chasing hens and getting stuck six inches apart. The roosters were screaming for relief. There it was *all before them* but they couldn't *reach* it!

Mohammed Maraka had got everybody in and around Barritos to go on strike. Even the high-bosomed armadillos at the Yacht Club. Cashew and Bratwurst were going bonkers—they had nowhere to drop their loose change.

The influence of Maraka was almost supernatural. He had no trouble with the Indians, or with the ignorance of the very under-privileged. He won them to his cause by promises of riches (natural-ly) and a good life better than they had ever dreamed. They were pushovers, and had everything to gain and nothing to lose. The oth-ers, sort of middle-class workers, had almost everything they want-ed—a house, a woman, a family, a donkey and a garden—and had been very satisfied until Mohammed Maraka came to give them *dreams.* A new Chevy pick-up, a washing machine, a vacuum cleaner, a whole set of Tupperware (without having to attend a party), a garbage compactor (and a year's supply of garbage), and so many other things. The way Maraka explained it to them they wouldn't have to do a thing to garner these treasures—just not work for a while.

This suited everybody just fine. Picketing was a novelty to these almost children of nature, and they enjoyed it to the nth degree, al-though the signs they carried were leftovers from other ''causes'' in labor's eternal struggle. The pickets at our place which included

113

Bobby and Timothy were carrying signs which read "Boycott California Grapes" and "Don't buy California lettuce" and "Reagan for Ambassador to Lebanon." It really didn't matter, I'm sure, because no one could read English, and if they could they had never heard of lettuce, California grapes or Reagan.

Some other signs appeared about this time, apparently provided by either groups or individuals who were going in business for themselves. Some of these messages were extremely esoteric, like "Maxie Rosenbloom died for our sins" and "Pope Paul is Anti-Mame." Then there were some signs carried by very odd looking people which contained simple messages like "José Madingo is a Pimp and an Episcopalian" and "Get money for your confessions, why tell everything for free?—Call Barritos 654 and ask for Father X, Y, or Z."

Hurd Cambridge was really in big trouble with this wildcat strike. His nuts were all over the ground and nobody was picking them up. He had a nut picking-up party one afternoon but it could hardly be called a success. After the first half hour everybody was so drunk they were picking the nuts up all right, but they were picking them up and throwing them at each other. Poor Hurd, he was left holding two hundred bags (empty).

A committee consisting of all of the town's merchants, plantation owners and others who were not on strike, visited the Mayor, who was wearing his utmost Adolphe Menjou outfit in honor of our visit—striped trousers, cutaway coat, wing collar, bow tie and all—plus Adolphe's finely pointed wax mustache. Outside of this sartorial indulgence, Señor Cassares, his honor, had little to contribute except saying that he would send a message to Brasília—first thing next week.

"What about this week!" Cousin Shapiro wanted to know.

"It's already Tuesday," the Mayor said, "the week is all shot." He said this in Portuguese and Cousin Shapiro interpreted.

"Ask him," I suggested, "if he *ever* heard *anything* from Brasília!"

This brought on a long dialogue between Cousin Shapiro, the mayor, Hurd Cambridge and Claudio, my foreman, and when it had ended we learned that the mayor had heard from Brasília just once in seven years—they wanted to know who the mayor of Barritos was?

We could see that this was embarrassing to his honor so we got the hell out of his office and trooped down to the Yacht Club—even without the armadillos and their Playboy bulging bosoms it was still a good place to forget about a strike. Or anything else.

"Just who is this Mohammed Maraka?" Hurd Cambridge asked after having ordered our second round of drinks.

"Well," Cousin Shapiro said, "he ain't no Arab sheik from Kuwait!"

"He's just a trouble makin' black bastard who's been sent down here from some radical group in North America to screw up Brazil just a little more," contributed the Reverend Meech.

"How would that be possible?" Reiko asked, "Brazil is just about as screwed up as it's going to get."

'That's what you think, Little Girl," Elizabeth Cambridge said. "These revolutionary bastards can take every native we have around Barritos and turn him into a bloodthirsty murderer, and for nobody's good but their own. They want to take over Brazil, and there's no easier way than to get the peasants stirred up."

"You sound like Marie Antoinette," Hurd said.

"You'd better believe it, my dear Robespierre," Elizabeth said, "Let 'em eat avocadoes!" Elizabeth Cambridge was on her fourth double triple.

"I've been reading Lenin," I said, and stopped the party cold. They didn't know what was coming next. Was I going to try and convert them to the cause?????

"You mean," Mrs. Tooze said, "Lenin—the Russian—who killed the Czar and all that? *That* Lenin????"

"Yes," I said, "and it's pretty scary."

"You mean," asked Hurd, "if we don't join 'em?"

"No," I said, "Lenin explains how easy it is to start a riot—which can lead to a revolution."

There was a general sigh of relief and another quick ordering of another round—all doubles this time.

"All you have to do is scream something inflammatory in a crowd," I continued.

Nobody asked "Like what?" so I told them.

"Like 'Down with Henry Kissinger's wife—Imogene!'"

"Imogene?" Elizabeth Cambridge stopped drinking but very momentarily, "I thought her name was Hortense."

"Whatever," I said, "I'm just using her name to illustrate a point."

"Her name is 'Virgil,'" Mrs. Tooze contributed, then dropped forward onto the table, her face sinking slowly into a large bowl of clam dip. She didn't seem to be drowning so no one gave her anything like mouth to mouth resusitation or artificial respiration. They just turned their backs so they wouldn't have to look at her breathing clam dip, even though it was probably the first and only time that a human had successfully substituted clam dip for oxygen.

"Well," Mr. Tooze said, "this is all a big revelation to me, and I read all the news that's fit to print, but I didn't know that Henry Kissinger's wife went around starting revolutions and I'd like to go on record as saying that I think it's un-American."

"Hear! Hear!" Cousin Shapiro said, just as Mogo, the Pygmy, his seven small wives and his forty-nine teeny-tiny children passed our table, "It's our anniversary," Mogo said.

Nothing much was resolved in the Barritos Yacht Club, but some very profound pronouncements were made. Which no one remembered. The strike continued and when we got back to Casa La Bombas that night, our ancient Volkswagen got glued to our driveway. A river of latex was oozing downhill toward the Amazon. I could picture the one-hundred-and-three-year-old man and his three kids pasted right in the middle of the river, unable to sail down, up or sideways, and a Lindblad Tour stuck right next to them with Mr. Lindblad sitting high on the upper deck explaining the mysteries of the Amazon to his amazed tour group, who were also getting very hungry because they couldn't reach shore as the brochure had promised and have a "delicious Amazonian dish of baked piranha, delicately flavored with finely chopped Brazil nuts and served by the handmaidens of the Gods of the Andes" (these were the bosomy armadillos at the Barritos Yacht Club).

"What are we gonna do now, Papa?" Bobby always asked.

"Papa doesn't know," Reiko said, as always. Timothy was already doing what we had to do. He was slowly making his way up the driveway, like a trapped fly on a curl of flypaper.

"Timothy!" I yelled, "What are you doing?" A dumb question which called for a very obvious or snotty answer. I got both: "I'm trying out for the Olympics, Papa. What does it look like I'm doing?"

"I'm going to swat your ass when I catch you," I said.

"You hafta catch me first!" This goaded me into more action than necessary and when I got out of the car I immediately skidded and did a double flip and a half gainer and landed on my back. Needless to say, Timothy, Bobby and Reiko screamed with merriment and my tuxedo has never been the same. It hardened over night and it's standing in the living room now—like a suit of armor. I couldn't bear to throw it out, because I had bought it twenty-three years before at Eddie Schmidt's in Beverly Hills, and it was full of memories—and it had *very wide lapels* (I *knew* if I waited *long enough*).

22

The strike went on. And one day all of the town officials, the plantation owners, the shopkeepers, and others like Mr. and Mrs. Tooze, who had become part of the group by osmosis, were meeting to decide what to do to end it. Amicably if possible.

"I have an idea," Dr. Ramsey said, bouncing (naturally) up from the conference table. Everybody listened because any idea of Dr. Ramsey's was well worth looking at. "Why don't we give them what they want?"

"You mean," Hurd Cambridge said, "Chevy pick-ups and roads and little little doo-dads like that!"

"No," Dr. Ramsey said, "give them an extra cruzeiro a day, more hospitalization than the usual aspirin and enemas, and free movies every Saturday night—at the old opera house. You can't do any more than that. Or any less."

"What about Mohammed Maraka?" I said, "and that little black dwarf with the sharp knife?" I knew something should be done because the whole countryside was getting sticky with latex and rotten with fallen nuts, but I wasn't anxious to irritate anybody who had a black dwarf with a sharp knife.

"That's just it," Dr. Ramsey said, "Mohammed keeps referring to some large group like an army or a gang back somewhere in the bush that he'll bring in if we don't comply—but what proof we we have that such a group exists? Anybody go back in the bush to find out?"

"No," Hurd said, "and I don't think we're going to get anyone to volunteer for that kind of exploration—too goddamn many of those little bastards with the curare tipped blow-guns around. You get one of those poison arrows up your ass and—"

"Your ass has had it," Cousin Shapiro finished, surprising us all. No one thought that Cousin Shapiro was that diagnostic.

"Look," Hurd said, because the spotlight was off him for a moment, and he didn't appreciate that, being the biggest plantation owner in the Amazon Valley, "I don't think we can afford to be funny at the moment. I know I can't. We've got to do something, and do it fast! The ground around my trees is six inches deep in rotting nuts. I think we should appoint a volunteer to follow that little black dwarf into the bush and see where he goes and what he does and who he meets—"

"*Appoint* a volunteer?" Reiko said.

"Yeah," I agreed, "how the hell does that make him a volunteer? Why don't *you* follow the dwarf? You know these jungles around here better than anybody except an anaconda."

"*Another* anaconda," Elizabeth Cambridge added.

"Don't try to start anything, Liz, this is a serious meeting," Hurd said, lighting a long brown beautiful Cuban cigar. "You want me to follow the dwarf?" Hurd challenged. "Okay. I'll do it. And if I don't come back—" he added like Olivier at his peak.

"If you don't come back," Elizabeth said, "I'll alert Pete El Jaguar immediately."

Hurd gave Elizabeth a long—and not particularly soft—look.

"Do that," he said.

"That little black dwarf usually takes off for the bush about four P.M. just after siesta—he goes right by our place." I said.

"I'll be there," Hurd said, and ordered a round of drinks for himself—only.

It was getting dark when Hurd came back out of the bush, threw himself in our easiest chair and asked for a drink, which I mixed. He really needed it. I gave him a few moments, until I couldn't wait any longer, "Well?" I said.

Hurd looked at me for a long moment, then he laughed until I thought he'd have a stroke.

"My God," I finally managed to get in, "was it *that* funny?"

Hurd stopped to catch up to his breathing, "You know who that little black dwarf met out there in the bush?" he started to laugh again, then, "*Another little black dwarf!* There's just *two* of them! That's the gang—the army—the group. Those two and Maraka. They are gonna take over—the three of them . . ."

"What about weapons?" Bobby was catching on fast.

"Two switch knives. The other little black dwarf has one too, and that swagger stick Maraka has, the one he's always slapping against this thigh—for emphasis."

"No laser guns?" Timothy wanted to know (he'd seen them a few thousand times on *Star Trek*).

"No," Hurd said, "nothing like that."

"Well," Reiko said, always anxious to get on with any tragedy. "What are we gonna do now?"

Timothy reached for the telephone and started dialing.

"Who're you calling?" Bobby asked.

"Mr. Spock," Timothy said. "He'll know what to do—remember him, Bobby? He's the one with the pointy ears."

"I know who he is," Bobby said, impatiently, as all big brothers are with little brothers.

"All right! All right!" I said, just as impatient as all parents are with big brothers.

"So," Hurd said, "tomorrow, bright and early I think we should have a confrontation with Brother Mohammed."

"Are you sure?" I asked. "He may have thousands of little black dwarves running around out there in the jungle. They could suddenly descend on Barritos—like that—and do the Gulliver bit."

"What's the Gulliver bit?" Reiko wanted to know.

"You know," I said. "Like in *Gulliver's Travels* where Gulliver, who is a full-size man, falls asleep on this island and all these little teeny-tiny men tie him up and when he wakes up he's helpless."

"You know, Mommie," Timothy helped out, "like the Munchkins in *The Wizard of Oz*."

"Oh," Reiko said, "remember what Judy Garland said about the Munchkins when they were making that movie. She said they were drunk all the time and were always pinching her on the ass."

"What else could they pinch?" Bobby said. "They were only two feet tall."

"Yeah," I said, "Judy and the Munchkins. I remember writing for Judy and Bob Hope so long ago on his show, and her talks with Jack on the Paar show. My god she was funny! She saw life differently from anybody I've ever known."

"You knew Judy Garland?" Suddenly Hurd was fascinated.

"Papa knew everybody," Bobby said. Which was true, but it made me sound like I should be in the *World Almanac* under 1886 to 1912.

"Look," Hurd said, remembering his mission. "You call everybody and we'll meet tomorrow morning at nine at the Yacht Club and *no drinking*—and get ahold of Mohammed. Get him there under the pretext that we're gonna settle."

"Thanks for telling me how to do it," I said to Hurd. "I was going to call him and tell him to be there because we were going to chop off both of his thumbs for being a bad boy."

Nine o'clock at the Yacht Club—everybody was there promptly and everybody was drinking (it didn't pay to lay out any rules in Barritos).

Hurd Cambridge had a brief exchange with his wife, Elizabeth, which was both loud and vituperative and loving. For them life was just one long *Who's Afraid of Virginia Woolf*. With the volume turned up.

After the third drink, Mohammed Maraka strolled in followed by one black dwarf and his ready switchblade.

Hurd waited until he was seated (the dwarf standing in back and to the right of him), ordered him a tall cool drink, then with the most elaborate casualness I've seen, said, "So you want to settle the strike?"

Mohammed straightened perceptively, "I beg your pardon?" he said, half-Harlem and half-Oxford, with a dash of Edward G. Robinson and George Meany.

"You want to settle the strike? Am I correct in assuming this?" Hurd baited.

"Of course," Mohammed said (he was back to straight Oxford

now). "We must settle the strike or else—why would we all be here?"

"But," Elizabeth Cambridge said, "We're not all here. There's someone missing."

This, I could see, unnerved Mohammed slightly. He looked around to fathom exactly what or who Elizabeth meant, then regaining complete composure said, "I think all of the most important people are here. The people who are most involved. The people who stand to lose the most if the strike continues. Of course, it doesn't have to," he added quickly, "if we all completely agree to my extremely generous terms."

"Who sent you?" Cousin Shapiro was blunt. The words were like dum-dum bullets—they went in small but they came out big.

Mohammed narrowed his eyes, as if he had practiced this maneuver, just to be ready for such occasions. "I don't think," he said, "it would help our negotiation or really add anything if that were known. I have my instructions from, let us say, the highest source and I, of course, must carry them out to the letter."

"Of course," Hurd agreed quickly, then. "Where's the other midget nigger?"

The little black dwarf pushed the button on his switchblade and eight inches of a frighteningly-sharp piece of steel flipped out, flashing in the bright Amazon sun.

At that same moment, Cousin Shapiro stuck the muzzle of a 12 gauge sawed-off shotgun against the dwarf's left ear. No one moved. It was a (freeze-frame) tableau of a pre-action to a massacre. A small massacre. The dwarf dropped his knife and pinned his left sneaker to the floor.

"Wait till Mr. Meany hears about this," Mohammed said.

"I was thinking the same thing," Hurd Cambridge said. "What do you want me to tell him?"

"Maybe we can talk this over," Mohammed suggested in a tone that whined a little.

We never learned where Mohammed Maraka had come from or who sent him or if it was all his own idea, but the work force of Barritos was more than satisfied with their extra cruzeiro a day, more beds in the hospital (they now have seven), more aspirin, enemas, and the free movies—every Saturday night. It was always the same: Burt Lancaster in *Moses* or maybe it was Moses as Burt Lancaster—I never knew because I never went to see. Burt had snubbed me once in Hollywood, and us Apaches don't forget.

The last we saw of our Labor Leader and his great cause and his two black dwarfs, they were sitting on the afterdeck of the *Lola Falana* as it pulled away from the Barritos town dock and headed toward midstream of the roiling Amazon. We all stood on the dock, Reiko, Bobby, Timothy, Hurd, Elizabeth, Cousin Shapiro, Dr. Ramsey and the various Barritos officials and Yacht Club members waving good-bye. Mohammed and the two little blacks didn't seem too thrilled by this display of farewellness, and just as the *Lola Falana* swung around a bend in the great river they slowly raised their hands and thumbed their noses at us. Expertly, I felt.

23

I have exaggerated, of course, the extent of the latex flow during the "strike" but it was considerable, and it seemed like weeks before we had it all covered with dirt, leaves, branches, sand, and whatever else was handy, so we could walk without becoming trapped in the gummy mess.

The strike brought home to us that we were utterly dependent on the tree milkers, just as dependent as a dairy farmer is on his help. Cows, I guess, are a little more demanding than a rubber tree. A cow has to be milked twice a day—morning and night. I don't know what happens if you don't milk a cow twice a day, but it would seem that the poor thing would have to spend a lot of time sitting down and maybe if no one relieved her there would be an explosion because a cow's Gucci can only hold so much.

The rumor that Nelson Rockefeller was going to visit Barritos got stronger. He was supposed to come for the big yearly event in Barritos, the Festival of Rubber and Nuts, which doesn't have the ring of the "Carnival of Rio," but we had been assured (and warned) that it was a really fantastic experience and one I would never forget. This, to me, sounded ominous, but then again even a TV weather report in Connecticut predicting that tomorrow would bring spring-like weather sounded ominous to me, because from our experience, a Connecticut forecast of spring weather always brought on a repeat of the blizzard of '88 plus a furnace failure. But I hoped that maybe things would be different in Barritos where life was very casual and so far, very pleasant—if very nonprofitable.

I guess Barritos must be rumor prone, because a few days after the announcement of Rockefeller's coming, Bobby rushed into the ranchhouse living room during siesta with startling news.

"Papa! Mama! Guess what!???" Bobby was very loud and Papa and Mama were very soundly napping. I sprang to my feet like I was being manipulated by a drunken puppeteer. Reiko just mumbled and turned her face to the wall (Japanese are hard to rouse).

"Papa! Mama!" It was Timothy. "Guess what!"

"Wait a minute," I said, I wanted to set my psyche for tragedy or disaster or both. "Don't tell me—the rubber bug has killed all our trees. Right?"

"Better than that," Bobby said. "They're gonna make a movie in Barritos!"

With this Timothy started wailing, "I wanted to tell Papa!" Tears streaming down his face he aimed a vicious kung fu kick at Bobby's groin. Bobby moved his groin just in time.

By this time Reiko was awake, and after I quieted Timothy down and let him tell me too that they were going to make a movie in Barritos, "What kind of a movie?"

"Remember 'The African Queen'?" Bobby said.

"I remember a lot of queens in my day," I said. "But I don't remember too many black ones—"

"No! No!" Bobby was appalled and annoyed by my lack of movie lore. "The movie they made a long time ago with Humphrey Bogart and Katherine Hepburn."

"Yeah," Timothy said. "Bogie and Kate—"

"And they're going to remake it with—guess who?" Bobby said.

I acted like I was pondering, then "Barbra Streisand and Fonzie?"

Bobby laughed and so did Timothy. "Not Barbra Streisand!"

"Fonzie and Goldie Hawn," Timothy said.

"Jesus Christ!" I said.

"No, Papa," Timothy said. "They couldn't get him and besides he's not SAG."

"You been reading *Variety* again?" I asked Timothy.

"No. But I have," Bobby said, "I've been explaining it to Timothy."

"I wish you'd explain it to me," I said. "I've been reading it for 35 years. Now, what about this movie?"

"They're arriving today at the dock, Cousin Shapiro told us."

The whole town was at the dock, pushing and shoving like a subway platform group. Every once in a while someone would get shoved from the dock into the water, and most of the crowd made no noticeable move to help him. A few of the more compassionate shouted warnings that schools of piranha—those voracious little fish that can clean a cow down to bare bones in about fifteen seconds—abounded near the Barritos town dock. Luckily they must have just satisfied themselves on a whole cow somewhere because no one was even nibbled. One old lady drowned, but only because she unfortunately chose the wrong moment to fall off the dock into the water—it was just as the *Lola Falana* and its load of movie people hove into sight round the bend.

Everyone cheered, I'm sure no one knew why, except that it did break the monotony of life in Barritos where the second most popular hobby was siesta. Make that the third most popular—number two was alcoholism.

The movie people turned out to be a grim lot. Admittedly, at first glance Barritos didn't look like the fun capital of the Western World. They had tons of equipment, which they left for the hundred-and-three-year-old man and his three kids to unload, and then they headed for the Yacht Club, which they had spotted quick as a red-tailed hawk spots a slow rabbit. They swooped down on the place and after a few quick belts they loosened up somewhat. I knew the director, Greg Harrison, and he was glad to see a face he recognized. When I asked about Fonzie and Goldie Hawn he laughed like a banshee.

"Jesus!!!!! Even if we had them this picture would be a dog!"

I didn't quite understand, and Bobby and Timothy wanted to know where the hell Fonzie (who had grown into a great favorite) was?

"You mean Fonzie, where are you when we need you????" then Greg laughed again. "We don't have him. We have Señor Fonzago, he's a big movie star in Wopland. Rome. Then we have Goldie

Hawkins, a country and western. She almost made it on *Hee Haw*, but somebody figured she'd be better for pornos."

"You're gonna make 'The African Queen' as a porno?" I couldn't believe it. "What do you have Bogie and Kate do. Play it naked and screw in rhythm with that old steam engine on the *African Queen* all the way down the river?"

"No," Greg explained. "This movie is called 'The Amazon Queen,' and it has nothing to do with screwing. It won't make a dime."

"Then why the hell are you making it?"

"Educational TV—they'll give you money for anything. They con all these big companies and foundations into thinking they're educating the people, but what the hell. We all need the work."

I left Greg and his now happy crew (they were drinking very well and getting along great with the Bunny-armadillos and this location locale was beginning to look pretty good to them). We made arrangements for them all to come out to our plantation (this sounded good now, "our plantation") later and told them not to drink the water, which is good advice on any location—especially in the jungles, or at P. J. Clarke's.

Bobby and Timothy were disappointed that Fonzie (the real one) and Goldie Hawn didn't show up, but I reminded them that it was a lot better than sitting at home all the time watching "I Dream of La Cucaracha de las poco poco mucha las fragos," on television. Which was a repeat—*every day*.

Actually the movie company wasn't as much fun as Bobby and Timothy thought it was going to be, as anyone who knows anything about the way they shoot movies could have told them. I know from the personal experience of visiting friends on the Hollywood sound stages that it is the most enervating experience life can offer.

They shoot one line of dialogue at ten different angles and for every angle the lights must be changed. Also if it's a funny line of dialogue it loses any humor it may have had after the fourth or fifth take. That's when dear Bob Hope would shine and win the eternal gratitude of anyone connected with the shooting. Just when everybody was ready to throw up if they heard that funny line just one more time, Bob would change it and have everyone screaming with laughter. Tensions would melt and the new line (carefully calculated by the old fox) would stay and become part of the movie. And the old fox's part would get bigger and bigger.

The big thrill of the movie company soon became routine, and the rhythm of life in Barritos continued with its same slow beat. Things were still very quiet. Except at night. At the Yacht Club. Things had livened up there considerably. When the day was done the movie people turned from their monotonous creativity to riotous frolic, which seemed to include many fist fights. As the local dentist who had diplomas from seven dental colleges (all located in Tijuana, Mexico) said (in Portuguese), "I'm makin' a pot full of money in recapping and replacing." On the movie set, closeups had to be cut to a minimum. Even porno actors and actresses needed teeth—for some scenes.

But the movie and everything else was forgotten with the announcement that Dr. Momomoomoo, the local witch doctor, had thrown ten virgins into Iquitoas, the volcano, because he thought by doing so Dr. Ramsey and the voodoo magic of her condoms would be destroyed by Inukuwa, the god of the volcano.

Pancho Bocachica, the Chief of Barritos' police, brought the witch doctor in for questioning.

First off—he wanted to know where Dr. Momomoomoo had found ten virgins.

24

The time for the Barritos Festival of Rubber and Nuts was less than two weeks off. Someone on good authority, like the one-hundred-and-three-year-old man who had just sailed upriver from Belém, had heard at the Café Gloria from the good authority of a Chinese bartender that Nelson Rockefeller was due any minute. Why anybody thought that this was good authority is a moot question—which became more moot every day when we tried, or the Barritos Mayor tried, to call the U.S. Consul in Brasília. He always got the janitor, and the janitor said that in the four years he had worked at the consul's office he had never seen the consul, but if he ever saw him he'd send the fastest Indian messenger immediately—then he hung up. All of which made little difference because I don't believe there was an actual telephone hook-up between Brasília and Barritos. There *was* a thin blue line pencilled in on the map of Brazil where ITT *thought* it should go.

Rumor, then, was all we had in our small town in the loneliest jungle in the world, so we had to make do. Dr. Ramsey had high hopes that everything was true and Nelson was coming, and she'd be able to talk to him and convince him that she *would* accomplish her Brazilian mission—if she could only have a few months more time. She was scared to death that she would be recalled by the HEW before she convinced the natives that condoms were better than wild hickory nuts.

Bobby and Timothy were attending the Barritos schools, such as they were. Such as they were, their idea of a hot lunch program was a fried banana every other day. That's how poor they were. We felt that even if Bobby and Timothy didn't particularly care for fried bananas at least they were learning to speak Portuguese, which they didn't particularly care for either, but we also felt it would come in handy some day if they ever found themselves in a Lisbon restaurant at noon and they wanted to order a fried banana.

Our plantation was batting 1,000 percent in rubber production—32,000 acres of rubber trees each giving us four or five pounds of latex a year, without fail. This was an unbelievable grand total of 144,000,000 pounds of unprocessed goo, and I figured that the way things were going—and *not a rubber buyer in sight*—we'd soon need the rest of Brazil to store the stuff. All because of Sir Henry Wickham, the Benedict Arnold of Brazil.

Although it was strictly against the law of Brazil, Sir Henry Wickham, back in 1876, picked 70,000 seeds of the Havea Brasiliensis rubber tree and smuggled them out of the country in a specially made brassiere (he told the customs men he was a Russian weightlifter).

Sir Henry Wickham then proceeded from Brazil to Malaysia and the Dutch East Indies where he sneaky-planted his 70,000 rubber tree seeds. This was the nucleus of the millions upon millions of acres of rubber plantations now covering those regions, which, because of the great convenience in shipping and the cheaper, more plentiful labor, brought the rubber industry of Brazil to its knees.

World War II helped some when the Japanese grabbed the far east plantations, and Brazil rubber was in demand once again, but when the war ended and MacArthur returned, the Brazil rubber men left.

And this is what Reiko and I got ourselves into. We went here following the brilliant success of running a ski-resort hotel in Maine, where the first year there was no snow, and when in desperation we bought a snow-making machine, we discovered that it was the slowest snow-making machine in existence, making snow, flake by flake. But it was *genuine snow*. That was the guarantee we got with the machine—no two flakes were alike.

So that's how it went—from a Maine snowless ski resort to a Brazil rubber plantation which produced millions of tons of rubber that no one wanted. We kept thinking—if only we could figure some way of getting Jerry Ford to say a few kind words at Aspen or Vail about the joy of downhill skiing on *latex,* or the thrill of becoming an instant yo-yo when you try jumping.

But life went on. Hurd Cambridge harvested his nuts and sold them to Hershey. Cousin Shapiro ordered his Levi's and sold them to everybody, at the same time keeping a sharp eye out for Nazi war criminals who had escaped to Brazil. Anyone in a wheelchair was suspect. Cousin Shapiro figured they must be getting to about that age. As a lucrative sideline, Cousin Shapiro sold *armed* wheelchairs to retired senior citizens who lived in retirement homes, and who weren't too agreeable with their fellow citizens when it came time to decide which TV show they would watch at nine o'clock.

Despite his supposed role as a double agent (maybe even triple) Cousin Shapiro had very sharp business sense. Over the years in Brazil he had collected a tremendous inventory in surplus weapons—M-1 rifles, machine guns, .45 automatics, grenades, bazookas, mortars, and mortar shells—but he adjusted them beforehand so nothing worked. Pull the pin on a grenade and out popped a Japanese fan. If anybody wanted to start a revolution in Brazil, and that included everybody, Cousin Shapiro was ready to help them get started—just so long as there was no trouble.

There seemed to be a sudden influx of Cubans around Barritos. The rumor (started by them, I presume) was that they were running out of land to plant sugar cane and tobacco in Cuba, and they were looking for plantations or ranches or a few thousand fifty-foot lots suitable for these worthy projects. Why they all carried guns and knives and had suspicious bulges in odd places in their clothing was never explained.

Mr. Brown had grown bolder and now marched his "troops" right down the main street of the little town. The goose-stepping was explained away by quoting from the new *Boy Scout Handbook,* it was supposed to take the place of knot-tying because everyone was sick to death of knot-tying and what the hell good was it anyway? What good goose-stepping was never came up, if Mr. Brown could help it.

I felt that the entire political and social identity of Barritos was changing, and not for the better.

Even Pete El Jaguar, the "bandit," picked up a little more character and courage—supposedly after reading something in Millie and Bernie's *How To Be Your Own Best Friend*—and stuck up the Barritos post office. He got seventeen special delivery stamps and the postmistress who was eighty-three years old, whom he promptly pitched off the Barritos town dock into the jaws of a waiting alligator, who just as promptly brought her back to shore and coughed her up.

Pete El Jaguar was arrested and released on bail, and Pancho Bocachica murmured, "Very nice."

The Reverend Meech continued tirelessly with his good work among the unwary, always accompanied by dyed-blond Mato Grasso nun with the holy-watered breasts under her peek-a-boo habit. The Reverend Meech had made many converts. Time and time again.

Norma-Lee, the Reverend Meech's wife, had switched from whatever she had been before and was now Princess Margaret. She went everywhere in town, looking for Lord Snowden. Or anybody.

Mrs. Tooze was also always on the scene, going from door to door with her little basket of condom boxes asking the natives if they needed any. She never found out because no one ever opened their doors, or if they were caught with their door open, they'd hide in the parlor under a pig.

Pierre Leuthold, the Swiss, was still trying to gather enough data for his book on the mating habits of the South American Indian which he hoped would be another *Jaws* so far as sales were concerned, but he felt very frustrated because the continued interference of Dr. Ramsey and her campaign for continence—or at least—caution. Pierre felt that Veronica Ramsey was making the natives very self-conscious about sex (something they had not been before her arrival) and he wished she would wander out into the jungle someday and just never come back. He was even thinking of arranging it. I could tell from his attitude. This young man was unstable.

The guru Mahareshi Nepal, when he wasn't making up Brahmanic couplets or quoting Mohammed or Buddha, was getting loaded with the Reverend Meech, because as the Reverend Meech put it, they were in the same spiritual racket. Mahareshi Nepal didn't think this was quite true but after a few triples he didn't care, and kept on spouting quotes from Chairman Mao, the Reverend Moon, and Rodney Dangerfield to anyone who would listen. All the time he spent in Barritos no one ever listened. Or even heard.

"The world and all the things in it are valuable, but the most valuable thing in the world is a virtuous woman," the guru murmured to the person closest to him, and the person closest to him would move to be the furthest away from him.

It wasn't that anyone disliked the guru Mahareshi Nepal, they just didn't understand him. "Give the laborer his wage before his perspiration be dry." This was another quote from Mohammed. He tried this out on Hurd Cambridge one payday when Hurd was trying to figure out how everybody was going to get paid without bankrupting himself, and Hurd grabbed him by the throat, for which no one could blame him. The nut business is no fun game.

But whatever, life was continuing in Barritos, as in the rest of the world, no matter if the Rubber and Nut Festival and Nelson Rockefeller were due at the same time.

25

The night was very dark. There was no moon. Hurd Cambridge, his wife Elizabeth, both unusually silent, and Reiko and I were sitting on our patio. Conversation had ceased. We didn't seem to have much to talk about. Reiko lit a cigarette, and a big moth dashed into the lighter flame and shortened his life considerably.

"Why are we so quiet tonight?" Reiko said.

Hurd Cambridge coughed, softly, "I'm worried about Nelson Rockefeller."

"What's to worry about?" Elizabeth said. "He didn't get to be President and he tried."

"I don't think that's very nice," I said. "But I'll have to admit—*I* voted for Doris Day."

"That doesn't make any sense," Hurd said. "She wasn't even on the ballot."

"I don't care," I said. "In the first place, I've never made sense, and I don't intend to start now. Besides, all I meant was that if a book that tells the story of the life of Doris Day gets to be number one in the *Times'* bestseller list she should get some sort of recognition for *incongruity* alone. Who in the hell ever figured that all of America would be *that* interested in the life story of Doris Day???? Why not the life story of Herbie Schwartz—or Selma Wojciechowski?"

"What are *you* talking about?" Hurd was shouting. "Who the hell are Herbie Schwartz and Selma what-the-hell ever? *I* never heard of them!"

"And you never will," I said. "But don't you think it's unfair

134

that somebody should write about Doris Day and not Herbie Schwartz and Selma Wojciechowski? That's not American!''

"Holy Jesus," Hurd Cambridge said. "I try to talk seriously and what do I get from a crazy man like this? Look, Douglas, why don't you go back to Hollywood?''

"What?" I said, "and live out the rest of my days, unnoticed, un-loved, un-humped—"

"That's vulgar," Reiko said. "Very vulgar. Let's talk about Nelson Rockefeller.''

"That's vulgar, too," Elizabeth Cambridge said, then laughed like a disembodied Valkyrie and ended with a hiccup.

"We gotta protect Nelson," Hurd said. "There are too many dissident groups in town and they'll get more dissident when the Rubber and Nut Festival starts. Dissident and drunk.''

"What about the police," Reiko said.

"Christ! They're the most dissident of all—the side that's winning is the side they'll join.''

"What do you think these 'dissidents' might do with Nelson Rockefeller?''

"Well, down here kidnapping is a real hobby.''

"I don't think that would be too practical.''

"Why not?''

"What would they want to kidnap him for anyway?" I asked, "and which group would grab him? We got so many groups— Angolans, Cubans, Chinese, Russians, Brown's Nazis, Pete El Jaguar's bandits, Israelis—''

"Israelis. What the hell would they want him for?''

"Maybe he can sing. He could be a cantor.''

Dr. Ramsey had joined us. We couldn't see her in the pitch black of the Amazonian night, but we could smell her perfume, which was a most aphrodisiacal aroma. I finally came to the conclusion that what I smelled wasn't perfume at all—it was her. Whatever—it was like a breath of Spanish Fly by Revlon.

"Veronica?" Reiko said.

"Gee, you're the sneaky one," I said. "Where are you?" Reaching out and inadvertently brushing one of her breasts.

"Oh, I'm sorry," I said.

"What did you do?" Reiko said, sharply.

"He just touched me," Dr. Ramsey said. "Accidentally."

"Naturally," Reiko said.

"We were just discussing what will happen to Nelson Rockefeller when he gets here," I said, lighting a candle. A *bug* candle.

"What'll happen to me?" Dr. Ramsey wailed a little.

"Oh, for God's sakes," Hurd said. "He'll be just as susceptible to you as *all* the males are. You'll get all the time in the world for whatever the hell you're doing down here."

"I just hope he doesn't ask me *what* I'm doing down here. What I've *accomplished*. I don't think he'll be too thrilled with the answer. Oh why couldn't they have sent somebody like Wilbur Mills—"

"Yeah," Hurd laughed. "Wilbur Mills and his Ways and Means. They couldn't have picked a better man for that committee. He knew the ways and—"

"Hurd," Elizabeth said, "that's corny, for Chrissakes—and it was so long ago. Why don't you go back to Warren G. Harding or even JFK. According to those scandal sheets he slept with everybody except Jackie."

"Who told them that?"

"Jackie."

"You know, Doctor," I said to Veronica, feeling foolish every time I called this delicious dish 'Doctor.' "I don't think *you* are exactly in a position of positive safety here in Barritos."

"I don't understand," Dr. Ramsey said. "I'm just here to try and do my part to keep the world—alive!"

"Yes. But Hurd here, doesn't want you around—handing out your little rubber love covers. He wants field hands—nut pickers—"

"Oh, come on now, Jack, I'm not a fanatic and Veronica knows nothing will happen to her with me."

Elizabeth shrieked with laughter. It was time for a drink.

Hurd flared a little. "What the hell's the matter with you, Liz.

You like to be married to some queer who doesn't look at other women?''

"Jesus," Elizabeth said, "You don't *look*. You start undressing them—and not with your *eyes* bullshit.''

"That's sweet," I said, and Reiko looked at me like I was crazy.

"Why don't we get back to Nelson Rockefeller time," Reiko suggested. "He should be here tomorrow."

Immediately there was silence.

"Why tomorrow?" Hurd wanted to know.

"Tomorrow's the beginning of the Rubber and Nut Festival and I thought everybody said Mr. Rockefeller would be here for the opening day.''

"I thought we started to worry about me for a minute there," Dr. Ramsey said.

"Well, it makes two we have to worry about," I said.

"I still don't get it," Dr. Ramsey said. "Hurd here naturally wants bodies for his lousy nut trees—but who else would want to—''

"You want the list?" I said. "Pierre Leuthold, he doesn't want you around because you're scaring the bejesus out of the natives with your little rubber caps. You are freezing them up—inhibiting them. They can't knock one off in the cornfield on the spur of the moment like they used to. Then there's the Reverend Meech. He refuses to wear a condom when he converts someone to his church—whatever his church may be God only knows, and why God doesn't strike him dead God only knows. The guru Mahareshi Nepal, another horny converter. He hates you for the same reason. He's non-violent except in your case.''

"How about Mr. Brown?" Elizabeth asked.

"Yeah," I said. "He's another. You've caused them to ponder about sex so much he's having trouble getting volunteers for his brownshirts.''

"And Pete El Jaguar," Elizabeth said. "He's not too fond of you, either.''

"What did I ever do to him?"

"That's it," Elizabeth said. "You're the only one in Barritos he hasn't been able to knock over—it's murdering his manhood.''

"What do you mean, *she's* the only one in Barritos he hasn't been able to knock over??!!!!'' Hurd was on his feet grabbing Elizabeth's long, tawny mane, almost holding her up with it.

"Hurd,'' Elizabeth gritted between her teeth. "Relax! You know goddamn well he's never touched me!''

"How about you!?'' Hurd bellowed like a stuck bull. "Have you ever. . . .'' He stopped in mid-sentence. "Why should I ask. I've seen you do it.''

"It's nothing!'' Elizabeth bellowed right back.

"Then leave it alone so it won't become something!'' Hurd yelled back, "I'm gonna get drunk!'' He stomped off into our living room and its cozy little bar.

"That's an idea,'' I said. "Let's all solve our problems in the only way problems ever get solved.''

We all stomped into our living room and our cozy little bar.

26

After an hour or more in our cozy Casa Las Bombas bar, the conversation had changed quite a bit. We were talking about pleasant things. We started to dig back into the history of this delightful Amazonas town of Barritos. It was a short history—like a single beat in the symphony of time.

Hurd Cambridge was our authority, and it seemed that Barritos had only a short 15 years as the rubber capital of the world. From 1900 to 1915.

Fortunes were made, apparently, by anyone who dared that dangerous and long journey up the mighty and treacherous Amazon.

Anyone included everyone, from the owners of the vast plantations, who were called rubber barons, to the lowest of the lowly prostitutes who were called whores. At a time when the Southside Chicago hookers were charging fifty cents a trick, which might last 25 or 30 minutes, in Barritos, any good, and enduring hooker could make a hundred dollars an hour and service thirty or more rubber roustabouts if she didn't waste time on useless conversation. If they wanted a little useless conversation she could make another fifty (dollars).

When the rubber boom burst most of the barons went bust along with it, while the prosties wound up with a pot. Some of them went back to Chicago and started their own World's Fair. Some went to San Francisco and bought the Fairmont, the Palace and St. Francis hotels (or so the story goes).

Some of the prostitutes stayed right on in Barritos and married the former rubber barons and started all over again by switching from humping to hoeing (newly planted Brazil nut trees).

When the rubber boom was over, the fun and excitement were over, and Barritos settled down into the dust of memories. Some remembered the magnificent opera house, which had opened at the rubber boom's apogee with the Ballet Russe who, during their two week engagement, had all died of malaria and yellow fever. Some of them expired in midair during "Peter and the Wolf." A few ballet lovers thought "The Dying Swan" the most fun because the swan died first, leaving the rest of the cast to ad lib. They didn't know whether to dance around her or bury her. I understand that they finally just pulled a chorus boy over her and let her lie there. All this, of course, is hearsay, and hearsaying it sixty-one years later adds very little veracity.

The rough and ready operatic group who had founded the Barritos opera house thought it was hilarious, but from that day forward they changed the name to Loew's Barritos and showed only Mary Pickford movies.

Mary Pickford was very popular in Barritos because she had long blond curls and somehow she looked different from the local Barritos girls, some of whom had inserted disks in their mouths to stretch out their lower lips like the African Ubangis. They thought it made them pretty, but all it did was fan you when they talked.

Gradually, and I guess out of boredom, the Barritos Chamber of Commerce (they had one, surprisingly) decided to do something to put Barritos on the map, even if they had to stay awake to do it.

Barritos needed money and they just couldn't seem to raise it from taxes because most of the tax collectors, especially those who went from door to door, never came back. Or were never heard from again. Every so often a skeleton would turn up with the skull missing, and Pancho Bocachica, the chief of police, would say, "very nice" and dismiss the whole thing as the work of the local head hunters. Head hunting, of course, was illegal, "but what the hell—they have no TV," which was one of the other things Pancho Bocachica used to say (in Portuguese) when these unpleasant occurrences occurred—then he'd pop another lolly in his mouth—he had the habit long before Kojak. And that was that.

The concept of the Rubber and Nut Festival evolved slowly— very slowly, because it must be remembered Brazil invented the hammock—so the Barritos Festival of Rubber and Nuts—a smaller, but planned to be no less rowdy and raucus version of the Carnival in Rio (which was world famous)—evolved like the laying of a six-pound egg by a three-pound chicken. It seemed an endless undertaking, and no one agreed with anyone else as to just how and what was to be done to attract tourists from all over the world.

Some wanted to bring back bullfighting, which had been outlawed many years ago, but the Brazil Humane Society was against it unless the rules were changed so that the bull would be allowed to kill the matador and be awarded the matador's ears, and tail, and other smaller items.

Elizabeth Cambridge, who was on the Rubber and Nut Committee thought this would be vulgar and not "family hour" at all. Most of the women of Barritos agreed with her.

"How about balloons this year?" Señor Cassares, Barritos' Adolphe Menjou mayor suggested, "I remember once in Rio, when I was a little boy they had balloons—everybody likes balloons." The mayor's suggestion was accepted after some discussion and three stabbings. My impression was that the Chamber of Commerce of Barritos was taking this a little too seriously but being a relative newcomer I thought it prudent to keep my mouth shut. Besides I am allergic to stabbings—they make me bleed.

"We need ether," the Reverend Meech said.

"Ether?" Reiko said. "Why?"

"In Brazil," the Reverend Meech said, very high and mighty like it was the 11th commandment, "every carnival time has ether. They squirt it in each other's faces. Wow! Do they get high!"

"I don't like *that* idea at all," Reiko said. "There'll be a lot of children in the crowd. What about them?"

"I don't think we have to worry," Mrs. Tooze said, "Back in Fergus, Ohio, where we come from, Mr. Tooze and I, we were childhood sweethearts—" She let it hang there.

"Wait a minute," I said. "Is that all there is to the story? Back in Fergus, Ohio, you and Mr. Tooze were childhood sweethearts—what the hell has that got to do with ether?"

"That's how it all started," Mrs. Tooze said. "One night after the Friday night basketball game, they had a dance and a fun festival and the kids squirted ether at each other and a lot of girls got pregnant that night, after the fun festival.''

"Jesus Christ,'' Hurd Cambridge said, "Americans! Barbarians!''

"Yeah,'' Mrs. Tooze agreed. "Fergus High won that night—beat Chillocothe 34 to 32.''

"Then it's decided,'' Mayor Cassares said. "We have balloons and ether. Now what about maté? Shall we serve maté? (Maté is a South American tea, made from god knows what—but not tea.)

"What the hell!'' It was the very loud voice of Ricco Luciano, Jr., the proprietor of the Barritos Yacht Club, "I can't make a dime from serving maté! We're gonna serve booze and you make it sound like we're gonna give it away! We're gonna charge, and it's gonna cost them goddamn tourists a lot more than we charge to the locals.''

"Look, Junior,'' Hurd said, "we're not going to *gouge* anyone. We want these tourists that we haven't even got yet to come back—again and again.''

"What about girls?'' Junior suggested. "Maybe a few from Chicago, or Minneapolis. Lot of hookers from Minneapolis.''

"You mean,'' I said, "more hookers come from Minneapolis than other cities?''

"Seems that way,'' Ricco said. "Maybe there's no demand in Minneapolis.''

"I've been in Minneapolis,'' the Reverend Meech said. "I would think the demand would be tremendous. What the hell else is there to do?''

"Gee,'' Mrs. Tooze said, "That comes as a big surprise to me. Minneapolis looks like such a nice place on the *Mary Tyler Moore Show*.''

"Those are just movie sets,'' Mr. Tooze said.

"Oh,'' Mrs. Tooze said.

The overall blueprint for the Barritos Festival of Rubber and Nuts finally emerged as a well planned mess.

Nothing was actually nailed down except everyone in the Chamber of Commerce agreed that we did need publicity to inform the outside world that the Barritos Festival of Rubber and Nuts was something not to miss because you only go through life once and if you attend the Rubber and Nut Festival, etc., etc.

I suggested Mary Wells of Wells Whatever as our representative, knowing that we'd never be able to pay her fee, but why not ask anyway.

Mary wrote the Barritos Chamber of Commerce a lovely letter saying that she was just too busy learning to ride a Yamaha* to take on the account, but she wished us luck, etc.

Anyway—Mary Wells or not—the Barritos Festival of Rubber and Nuts was going to take place.

*What's a Yamaha?

27

At five A.M. on the first day of the Barritos Festival of Rubber and Nuts, the whole town and all of the surrounding countryside were aroused from sound sleep by the screaming steam whistle of the good ship *Lola Falana.* She was in midstream, at the end of her long journey up river from Belém, announcing to the waiting world that she was ready to dock.

Usually, no one in Barritos gave a damn whether the *Lola Falana* was back from Belém or not—unless you'd sent for something from Sears, or the Mother Cabrini Cocktail-of-the-Month Club. Today was different. Suddenly a series of explosions like the beginning and end of World War II demoralized everyone, until we realized they were just firecrackers smuggled in from South Carolina (where our cigarettes come from). These firecrackers must have been special because they out-cherried any cherry bomb I'd ever heard. Windows blew in (and out) all over town, making everyone laugh and laugh and laugh, unless, of course, you happened to get a little sliver of glass through your nose. Or your ears pierced (from one side of your head to the other).

The *Lola Falana* had a small field piece mounted on her foredeck in case she should meet with some river pirates and the one-hundred-dred-and-three-year-old man, who was owner, skipper, and gunnery officer of the riverboat, was amusing himself by firing this unformidable weapon directly at Barritos. This bombardment of the undefensible town of Barritos was inadvertent. To the one-hundred-and-three-year-old man, one direction was the same as any other. His eyesight was so poor, he could no longer distinguish the difference between light and dark. With him it was either dark—or darker.

How he piloted the *Lola Falana* up stream through all those thousands of shifting sandbars from Belém to Barritos was unexplainable unless he was part bat with built-in radar. Looking at his wizened, mishapen form he could have been part *anything*. Finally he got tired, or ran out of ammunition just after he had knicked the steeple on the Reverend Meech's house of worship and other things so Barritos was safe until the landing of the *Lola Falana* at the town dock. This was always either a disaster soon to be revealed or a near-miss to thank God over.

The hundred-and-three-year-old man pointed the river boat somewhere in the direction of the place where he thought the Barritos town dock should be, then he revved up the ancient engine till its flywheel became something to be reckoned with. If it had ever let go it would have sliced the *Lola Falana* in half and the hundred-and-three-year-old skipper right along with it, because the flywheel was directly under the wheelhouse and more directly right under the skipper.

People, chickens, dogs, cats, pigeons, gulls, rats and fish ran, flew, swam, and scrambled for their lives as the *Lola Falana* whacked full steam ahead into the main town dock at a ninety-degree angle and mangled the seven old Dodge truck tires the skipper had skewered to the bow for battering-ram purposes. He knew he wasn't the navigator he once was. Or ever was. They say that when he was twenty-six-years-old he piloted the *Lola Falana* right into the main dining room of the Café Gloria in Belém—killing a whole Seder.

The bow of the *Lola* stayed where it was, as the Amazon's current shoved the stern against the dock, at which point the hundred-and-three-year-old man's three nimble sons made her fast.

No one, so far, had seen Nelson Rockefeller. We thought maybe he was going to make an entrance, but there were quite a few other tourists and the decks were crowded unmercifully with crates (some of which looked like the same crates that Dr. Ramsey's condoms had arrived in—almost a year before). There were also a lot of other crates that looked like the ammo boxes we had seen at Cousin Shapiro's Army & Navy store.

After the tourists, who were not too young and looked very weary, had sorted out their luggage with no help from any of the *Lola*'s crew, they trudged up the knot-holed gangplank toward the Barritos Hilton.

But still there appeared no Rockefeller or anyone who looked like he or she might be part of his entourage. Everyone was standing around in little groups, looking at each other with unasked questions.

"Well, where the hell is he?" Hurd Cambridge finally wanted to know. "I hope the hell we haven't fixed our bedroom up into the 'Presidential Suite' just to have it sit there with no Nelson Rockefeller in it!"

"Let's have a look below decks," I suggested. We did this. It didn't take long. There was only one section which could have been called a stateroom (if you had a wild imagination), but there was no one visible. I even checked the head and the closets. Nothing.

Back topside, the crowds were thinning out on the dock, when I noticed a black shoe, with a foot apparently in it sticking out from behind a crate of fresh canned fruit. Hurd saw the foot at the same moment and gave it a tentative kick. The foot was withdrawn and a whole man appeared. He had been sleeping back there in the shade. He was the most crumpled individual I've seen. His white wash-and-wear suit looked like it had been ironed sometime around the turn of the century by someone who had never seen cloth before.

His necktie was multicolored, as is the fashion today, and I had the feeling that the knot in it had never been untied after the first time. His shirt was bluish and unbuttoned and his hat could have been also used for a barf bag. He hiccupped, three times.

"Hi—there—I'm," there seemed to be a long time between words, "I'm Congressman Hammond—of Minnesota."

"How do you do," Hurd said. "Welcome to Barritos. May I help you with your luggage?"

"My luggage?" Congressman Hammond seemed out of it for the moment.

"Yes," Hurd persisted. "You know—your bags and stuff."

"Oh, bags and stuff," the congressman repeated, then repeated again, "—bags and stuff."

I felt I had to help out here. "Are you new in Minnesota?" I asked.

"Oh," the congressman said, taking advantage of an opportunity to become hilariously witty, "I'm about the same in Minnesota as I am here. Bags and stuff." He started looking behind crates.

"Are you in the House of Representatives?" I had to know. He didn't look like he was in the house of anything.

"You're goddamn right!" he said, "Representative Harry L. Hammond—Minnesota."

"Whatever happened to Rockefeller?—he was supposed to be—"

"What *could* happen to him?—he's *loaded!*" Hammond said. He started to shove a few crates and boxes back and forth, not really accomplishing too much.

"Don't seem to be any bags and stuff," he announced with a great deal of finality. "Shall we go wherever we're going. Maybe to a bar?"

"Something wrong here," I sotto voce'd to Hurd.

The Congressman overheard me, and said, "Nothing wrong. I represent the twelfth district of Minnesota, in the congress. Is that a crime?"

"I don't know," Hurd said. "I've never been there."

"Great state," Congressman Hammond said. "Cold as a bitch."

"You know Nelson Rockefeller?" I asked.

"Yeah," he said. "He suggested that I come down here and take care of things."

"Like what?"

"I dunno—*you* tell *me*—and I'll take care of *things.*" Then, "No bags and stuff. Musta left them at the airport," then he hiccupped, "in Minneapolis."

So, I thought to myself, this is what they send down here to Brazil to take care of things.

"Is that a bar over there?" Representative Hammond wanted to know, pointing more or less in the direction of the Barritos Yacht Club.

"It sure is," I said.

"What *things?*" Hurd persisted.

"Is—er—Dr. Ramsey still around?" Representative Hammond asked.

"Oh," Hurd said.

28

The Festival of Rubber and Nuts in Barritos was patterned after the original Carnival in Rio, which has now become so commercial and touristy it has lost most of its innocence and spontaneity.

The Festival in Barritos was certainly spontaneous, not due to any lack of planning, but due to the addition of alcohol to the samba. This put Barritos one up on Rio, because surprisingly the Carnival in Rio is comparatively sober. I'm told that only the squirting of scented ether in each other's faces at the Rio Carnival produced anything like intemperate behavior—such as the young Cariocans peeing on the crowd below from a cornice of an on-the-beach hotel, a feat which was usually applauded by the jovial recipients.

The Barritos Festival of Rubber and Nuts started as all festivals do with a parade led by the Barritos Town band which consisted of sixty-three bass horns and one fife. The reason for the overabundance of bass horns was a simple one. They were big and brassy and made horrendous noises, which appealed very much to the citizens of Barritos. The lone fife player was an introvert and lived in a closet in the house of his sister. I guess he could be called a closet fife player. The effect created by the sixty-three bass horns playing along with the fife was that of a herd of elephants trying to stomp a mouse, but this musical aggregation was very popular in Barritos because they always played during the fights at the weekly *futebol* games between the Barritos All-Stars versus the Manaus Angels, the Iquitos Dodgers, the Mato Grasso Mets, or some other team in the Amazonas league. A word about *futebol* in South America. It is taken very seriously. The fans are described in a Time-Life book as "cheerfully" bellicose. Apparently they are more bellicose than cheerful because besides soft drinks and a variety of hot dogs, vendors pass among the crowds hawking vicious looking long-bladed knives, "Hee-yah! Getcha switchblades for after the game!!!!"

But there was no bellicosity in Barritos, not on this long-awaited day of festival and fun. There should have been some, considering the way every male was getting chummy with every other male's wife or daughter or grandmother or grandfather (we had a few old gay grandfathers in Barritos as elsewhere) but no one seemed to mind in the least. It was a replay of the German Oktoberfest in Munich only with a samba beat. And with more passion and less grunting.

At the Barritos town square, a beautiful place of many-colored inlaid tile streets, fountains of fantastic design shot sprays of icy mountain waters in all directions, between the groups of huge and ancient Jacaranda trees whose purple blossoms perfumed the air with their subtle suggestive aroma. It was here in the middle of the beautiful town square that the sixty-three big brass bass-horned Barritos town band stopped—abruptly! They had accidentally marched right over the fife player. He never should have stopped to pull up his sox.

The suddenly vast population of Barritos and the surrounding countryside was rapidly filling the town square. They didn't want to miss the "BIG SURPRISE," although they didn't know what the "BIG SURPRISE" was going to be. They soon found out. It was Dr. Veronica Ramsey, outfitted in the very least of a string bikini, running through the mob, distributing little "BIG SURPRISE" purple boxes of Ramses, Trojans, and something new called "Warren Beatty's," which despite wild rumors in Hollywood were not part of the Universal Movieland Tour.

These little "BIG SURPRISE" gifts were not received with any great enthusiasm by the now huge crowd in the Barritos town square, but Dr. Ramsey's bikini made a tremendous impression and when she finally tore herself away from the mob she had very little of it left.

Up until now she had managed to elude Congressman Harry L. Hammond and his amorous advances, all of which kept her moving at a rapid pace because the congressman was like a ferret in heat. He searched everywhere for Veronica except the men's room at the Yacht Club where Ricco Luciano, Jr., had kindly consented to keep her locked up with an OUT OF ORDER sign on the door.

Dr. Ramsey, happy with her luck so far, later ducked out a side door and ran into the one-hundred-and-three-year-old man, who made a gesture of admiring her bosoms and murmured to himself, "Cheech and Chong."

"You're a dirty old man," Dr. Ramsey laughed.

"Why not?" said the Dirty Old Man, "I've tried everything else."

As Cousin Shapiro told me later, all the while the Barritos town band was scaring the shit out of every living thing for 39 miles around, including the Howler Monkeys, who were howling louder than ever and running for their lives, the various little "revolutionary" groups were having their little revolutionary meetings all over town.

Mr. (Field Marshal) Brown (Braun) was drilling his troops back in the jungle close by the Bridal Veil Falls, and finding it very difficult to get them to goosestep in what turned out to be a swamp with lots of leeches and a small alligator here and there. But Herr Braun (Brown) was a strict disciplinarian and anybody who did not obey his loud teutonic commands was immediately shot—in theory anyway. He couldn't really shoot anybody because his army was small enough as it was, and if he was planning to take over Brazil's 3,286,470 square miles of territory and its population of 107,661,000, he'd better not shoot anyone. It might make the difference between success and failure.

I don't know how Cousin Shapiro's grapevine worked so well, but he gave me the inside on the Cubans, too. They were meeting in another part of the jungle. They were ready to get the "move-in" signal from Castro. The move-in time was to be at midnight of the third and last day of the Barritos Festival of Rubber and Nuts and the takeover point was to be the Hacienda of Hurd Cambridge where Hurd would be giving a huge celebration party in honor of Nelson Rockefeller, who was elsewhere, but Hurd was going ahead with the party anyway. He figured that nobody in Barritos knew what former Vice-President Rockefeller looked like anyway so he let them all believe that Congressman Hammond was the former Vice-President. What could it hurt?

After a quick conference the Barritos town band decided that one lousy fife player was not too necessary in a band of 63 bass horns and he would not be missed except by his sister and his dog who used to bite him a lot because the dog hated the stuff the fife player kept bringing home in doggie bags. The dog just didn't like pizza and that was that.

Just as the Barritos town band struck up that week's Brazil National Anthem, Cousin Shapiro snuck up behind me and whispered, "They're here."

"Who's here?" I said. Although I certainly didn't want to know. "Chou En Lai and his army—paratroops."

"Oh come on," I said to Cousin Shapiro, tired of all this crazy South American intrigue.

"Chou En Lai is dead—he's been dead for a year."

"I know," Cousin Shapiro said. "But he just came from the taxidermist and he looks great."

"What about Mao Tse-tung. Is he joining us, too?" I was not nice.

"He's still at the taxidermist—maybe later." Cousin Shapiro went right along.

"Okay," I said. "I give up. What are the Chinese doing here in Brazil?"

"The Russians are here, too."

"Russians in Barritos. To do what?"

"They ain't here to pick nuts," Cousin Shapiro said.

The Barritos town band had concluded the Brazil National Anthem and started playing "Tiptoe Through the Tulips" and if you haven't heard "Tiptoe" played on 63 bass horns, you've lived a full rich life.

"Are the Russians paratroopers, too?" I asked.

"No. They been living here. Claudio, your foreman, his real name is Vladimir Ivanovitch. He's a General."

"Look, Cousin Shapiro," I said, "are you telling me all this just to lighten my day, because you know, my days are light enough because I'm a Jehovah's Witness *and* an Episcopalian, and if my Rabbi gives the word. . . . Also, I don't need any more plot at the moment.''

"Hold it, Jack," Cousin Shapiro said. "Let's not forget the Reverend Meech, the guru Mahareshi Nepal, Pierre Leuthold, King Mogo of the Pygmies, Pancho Bocachica, Pete El Jaguar, and Elizabeth Cambridge—''

"Elizabeth Cambridge. She wants to take over Brazil?"

"No. She wants to get rid of Dr. Ramsey. Liz has been hearing stories about her and Hurd."

"That's ridiculous," I said, finding myself getting overheated with jealousy even though I knew that any rumors like this were absolutely false.

"Try and convince Elizabeth Cambridge of that—she even bought a Baretta .38. It's a little Italian pistol that's got the wallop of a—''

"I hope she's a good shot," I shouted, as the Barritos town band crashed into "Boola, Boola" and "Fight On, Wisconsin" simultaneously.

"She's gonna need a good *lawyer!*" Cousin Shapiro screamed back.

"I got *just* the *man*," I said, as the band lost interest in music or whatever they thought they were doing and stopped playing entirely. "Ed Poochie of Liverwurst Falls, Maine—or some town with a name like that—''

"Ed—*Poochie?*" Cousin Shapiro said, without much faith.

"Yes," I said, "That's the way the people in Maine pronounce it—he's some kind of French-Canadian or something, and that's as close as they can get to the correct pronunciation of his name, but he's a *doll*—fat and jolly—some of the people up there in Maine *really believe* in him—*because* he's fat and jolly. And boy! Can he fool those judges up there. Somehow *they* believe in him—again I suppose because he's fat and jolly. I saw him frame a guy one day— his own client—got the judge to find *him*—his *own client*—in contempt of court. What a sense of humor! But I like him—He's such a charlatan. Drinks pretty good, too, and starts fights in saloons. He slugged a friend of mine one Saturday night just because my friend happened to mention another Maine lawyer—Joe Fulman, who just got disbarred for something or other—I think it made Poochie nervous. Or maybe it's his mother. He lives with his mother. Maybe *she* makes him nervous.

"I don't think Elizabeth Hurd would be very happy with a nervous lawyer—especially if she shot her husband," Cousin Shapiro suggested.

"But that's the *point*," I said, "It would liven up any murder trial if you had a lawyer like Poochie defending you—he's liable to take either side—keep you guessing until the last minute whether you're going to get hanged or shot."

"Douglas," Cousin Shapiro said, "You'd be a smash entertaining the boys in the Death House. Why don't you arrange a tour?"

29

The Barritos Festival of Rubber and Nuts ran its full three days, but the second day was as nothing. No man, woman, child, dog, cat, chicken, pig, or bug moved. They couldn't. It was a day long to be remembered in Brazil's history, and it was to be called "The Day of the Barritos Hangover." Only the witch doctor, Doctor Momomoomoo, was able to have any kind of constructive thought. He thought it would be a marvelous day for a human sacrifice. His.

What had happened I learned from my most reliable source of information, Cousin Shapiro. He was not only reliable, he was almost like a permanent guest at our little Hacienda. So much so that one day I had to ask, "Who's watching the store?"

"Buddha," Cousin Shapiro said, looking like an Oriental Puck.

"Is he any good?"

"He can't make change."

"Too bad," I said.

"Yeah," Cousin Shapiro said, "and he just joined the Teamsters Union."

"No shit?"

"Plenty," Cousin Shapiro said, "from them—if you don't do what they say."

"Where is everybody?" I wanted to know. "It's only the second day of the Festival!"

"Well," Cousin Shapiro said. "It's a long story."

"Then skip it," I said. "This is my day to try and figure out the Brazil income tax."

"That takes two minutes. Just take the tax form, write across the top of it 'Sorry. Mister Douglas was killed by a plutonium fart' then send it back. By the time they figure *that* out you can be in Peru—or Venezuela—or any country, which doesn't have extradition.''

"You sound like Vesco.''

"I'm his tax man,'' Cousin Shapiro said, and I'll never know whether he was kidding.

"Look, tell me what happened downtown—it's so quiet—and make it short,'' I said.

"Yesterday,'' Cousin Shapiro began. "After the Barritos Festival of Rubber and Nuts got going real strong, somebody thought it would be a good idea to have a little drinkee.''

"Drinkee????'' I couldn't believe this was coming from Cousin Shapiro.

"They wanted to get drunk.''

"That's better.''

"So they took over the Barritos Yacht Club and drank it dry. You should see downtown, people lying all over the place sleeping it off—they were even giving it to dogs, cats—anything!''

"I'll go down later,'' I said, "You know, take the little woman and the kids. They don't get to go much.''

"Yeah,'' Cousin Shapiro said. "Jack, you're a real *father!*'' He said 'father' but he made it sound like 'mother'.

"What about all the little revolutionary kidnap groups. What happened to them?''

"They all got drunk, together. They're all on the same side now.''

"The Cubans, Chinese, Angolans, Israelis, Nazis and the Teamsters—all of the same side? Who they gonna fight?'' I was feeling more perturbed now than at any previous time. Before the whole thing seemed like the same old South American bloodless coups where no one actually won, but if they were all on the same side, who would they attack? Could be the innocent bystanders—us.

"Big party tomorrow night.'' Cousin Shapiro changed subjects abruptly.

"More drinking?'' I asked, foolishly.

"Ho! Ho! Ho!'' Cousin Shapiro said. I knew this meant yes.

Hurd Cambridge was a great party giver and he *never* ran out of booze. I think he had a secret Swiss bank account filled with nothing but secret booze.

"Who's gonna be the guest of honor?" I said. "They don't have Nelson Rockefeller."

"They don't know that. People around here—"

"What does that mean?"

"They think Congressman Hammond is Rockefeller."

"Oh," I said. "Then maybe somebody'll kidnap Hammond and Dr. Ramsey's troubles would be over. She wouldn't have to hide anymore."

"Congressman Hammond is the head of the Condom Committee in Congress. If he disappears there'll be no more condoms for Dr. Ramsey, and at the rate the natives are using them up, for the wrong purposes, she's gonna need plenty more if she wants to conquer this over-population problem."

"Well," I said, "We'll have to tell them that Harry L. Hammond isn't Nelson Rockefeller."

"Maybe they'll kidnap him anyway."

"Jesus! Who'd pay the ransom?"

There was a period of silence after this that lasted all afternoon.

The second day of the Barritos Festival of Rubber and Nuts finally passed. Many of its citizens who had wished to die quickly the day before woke up fully refreshed and ready for another day of celebration, their ghastly hangovers conveniently forgotten. People who had prayed for forgiveness the day before now prayed for a jug and a girl. Or a boy.

The Barritos town band, now down to 36 big brass bass horns, played another version of the Brazil National anthem. This time it sounded like "The Girl from Ipanema," which is still a very popular melody in Rio de Janeiro where the girls from Ipanema go to the Cococabana beach dressed in three pieces of string (if you're counting), and a little protective Coppertone (which makes them very slippery).

The fife player was back, playing "Yankee Doodle" now, no

matter what the others were playing. With that bloody bandage on his head he figured what else?

Dr. Ramsey's multi-colored condoms were being blown up into pretty balloons, breaking Dr. Ramsey's heart but winning the undying devotion of balloon lovers everywhere.

The ancient cannon in old Fort Barritos was fired—just once. Once was enough to blast it into a thousand pieces and cut the gun crew into neat rows of sliced catfish bait—which just happened to be in short supply. Funny the way fate just seems to step in at the right moment when things look the blackest.

The drinking started once more at the Yacht Club and Ricco Luciano, Jr., became his old morose self, almost; for the Festival he *had* stopped threatening every one who displeased him with the Black Hand, and worse. This was his way of entering into the spirit of things.

Field Marshal Braun held several parades up and down Main Street. His group wore their make-shift German army uniforms, but their goose-step was reminiscent of a strut to "Way Down Yonder In New Orleans." A few times, some of the ambitious (or maybe warlike) Angolans joined the "German army." Their goosestep looked like a bunch of Navajos praying for rain and their color didn't match anybody's—they were black as our American blacks *used* to be (before Adam Clayton Powell told them to cut down).

The Cuban army, the Chinese army, and the Russian army, who were very few in number, also marched, but down Main Street in the opposite direction. When Field Marshal Braun's army met the other armies at the corner of Main and Elm it looked like trouble, but by some terrific coincidence the Barritos Yacht Club just happened to be at the corner of Main and Elm, and after a very military sounding and looking conference everybody in all the armies adjourned to Ricco's bar. From then on things were quiet except for an occasional burst of machine gun fire from inside—which took off a few shingles on the outside.

I thought the whole Barritos Festival of Rubber and Nuts and Revolution had begun to take on the air of a Gilbert and Sullivan operetta as presented by the West Sedalia, Missouri, Sedentary

Spastic Players to help the people of West Sedalia, Missouri, forget for a moment, that they were living in West Sedalia, Missouri.

And that's the way it was in Barritos, Brazil on the night of February 18, 1977.

30

There was no twilight the night of the Hurd Cambridge's Fantastic Fun Festival to top off the Barritos Rubber and Nuts Celebration. There was no sunset. It was day—then suddenly it was night. A very dark night. The blackness rolled over the mountains, the hills, the groves of nuts, rubber, vanilla, and cocoa like a final tidal wave. Here and there, barely visible, wispy trails of blue-grey smoke drifted over the native huts, and deep in the valleys and on the sides of the gentle hills was the soft yellow glow of bug lights which surrounded the patios of the large plantation houses. These mixed with thousands of tiny dots of the lighted candles of Macumba. Macumba—a highly developed native religion based principally on voodoo.

This extraordinary display of white or black candles—the color depended on whether it was good or bad magic the natives were trying to produce—had apparently been brought on by the sudden night. The natives were sure that there had been a meaning in it and that some unknown danger was approaching under the cover of this thick black darkness. The drums, the wailing and the chicken sacrifices were going strong. According to some of the stories I had heard from Cousin Shapiro, these voodoo believers had often been right.

I had the feeling as Reiko and I were driving out to the Cambridge Plantation that I had never seen *darkness* before this night. The lights of the car made no shadows.

Remembering the first time we had driven out to Cambridge's, when we had run into the giant anaconda hanging down from a tree over the road, I kept a sharp eye out and sure enough we ran into him again.

He dropped down onto the hood of our little car with a tremendous thump! I just knew we'd never be able to get the hood up again. The anaconda had more poise than we had. Reiko and I were in the back seat screaming, while he just gathered his thousands of coils together and slithered down off the hood, to the ground and up the tree again, presumably to wait for the next car. This seemed like a strange hobby—even for a snake.

We were still quivering when we pulled up the Cambridge's flaming torch-lined driveway. There must have been hundreds of torches and the effect was always breathtaking. Like someone once said, "They sure know how to waste oil."

The Cambridge bash was to be a costume party and a man who looked like a Watusi, only taller, who was dressed like an Eighteenth Century butler, admitted us and announced us over a loud speaker. "Jack Douglas and his Lovely wife, Reiko, directly from the Las Bombas Rubber Plantation." It was like being on with Merv, or Johnny or Mike, or Barbara Walters. We were thrilled until the Watusi added, "Brazilian rubber prices dropped to a new low today on the New York Stock Exchange. Minus 6.8."

"Thanks," I said "for the good news."

"Remember *me*," he said. "I used to be 'Farina' in the *Our Gang* comedies?" He stuck out his outsized hand. I shook it.

"I remember you very well," I said, looking up at his full seven feet six inches. "You used to be taller."

"Yeah," he laughed, and slapped my outstretched palm. "Glad to have you aboard, boy!"

"Who's he?" Reiko asked.

"I don't know," I said.

"You acted like you knew him."

"That's show business," I said. "You gotta act like you know *everybody*."

"Why?" Reiko asked.

"You know," I said. "I never found that out. It's like that 'The Show Must Go On' bit. *Why?*"

"Jack," Reiko said, "I don't have the slightest idea of what you're talking about, but it's *very interesting.*"

"Thank you," I said. "And you're getting to be a pretty snippy little Jap."

Elizabeth Cambridge broke through the enormous crowd in the Cambridge Hacienda's Grand Ballroom like a Notre Dame running back, and greeted Reiko and me. "So nice of you to come," she said. "So very fucking nice."

"It's a pleasure," I said. "A fucking pleasure."

"Please," the Reverend Meech said, who was passing at that moment. "Please, no fucking profanity. Not while the Reverend Meech is tending to his flock." He hurried on toward Dr. Ramsey's cleavage, which he had just spotted.

"Dear sweet man, the Reverend," murmured Elizabeth and disappeared into what looked like the back of an ostrich, but it was Mrs. Tooze's best party dress. She was supposed to be Marie Antoinette—or Louis XIV. *Mr.* Tooze was dressed like Tarzan, with his fly open.

The rest of the costumes at the party resembled the costumes Truman Capote urged for the "April in Paris" Ball, or maybe the Artists and Models ball they used to have somewhere in the Village, that gave the Gays the opportunity of a lifetime to dazzle without the risk of being arrested—except on the subway, going home in the morning.

Cousin Shapiro came to the party as Tony Curtis as Yul Brynner's son in *Ghengis Kahn.* He spoke Chinese with a Brooklyn accent. Three men came as Howard Hughes and Cousin Shapiro whispered to me, "How do we know they aren't?"

Hurd Cambridge, the host, was dressed as Henry VIII, and spent a good deal of the evening gnawing on bones which always seemed to be attached to tasty young girls.

Pete El Jaguar came as Muhammad Ali in a boxer's training outfit, complete with a leather-covered aluminum cup, which frustrated Elizabeth Cambridge to the point of tears. Maybe El Jaguar was growing tired of her using it like a leash, or maybe he had other plans for the evening. Whatever, the chief of police, Pancho Bocachica, got a little drunk and tried (for reasons known only to him) to arrest Pete. He soon found himself handcuffed (with his own private handcuffs) to a bed post in the Presidential Suite. Half sitting and half standing. He said later it was the longest party he had ever attended, and he would never advise Pete El Jaguar of his rights again.

There were at least 56 Richard Nixons attending the party—all doing their Rich Little impersonations. Two impersonators of Woodward and Bernstein were there taking notes and asking everybody questions. They felt they might get a whole new book of inside secrets out of somebody who could do a good impression of Nixon.

"Funny," Cousin Shapiro said. "Nixon is the only one who can't do a good impersonation of Nixon."

I couldn't figure that one out, but I found myself liking it.

The Cambridges had outdone themselves on this party; Bobby Short was at the piano, entertaining his little heart out. No one was paying any attention to him because no one in Brazil had ever heard of him except a little Jewish couple who had once made a pilgrimage to New York's Carlyle Hotel to hear him. They applauded everything he played. They even applauded when he didn't play. Finally about eleven P.M., Bobby asked them to stop. They didn't, so Bobby told them if they didn't stop overdoing it he would cut off his hands. They didn't stop and you can guess the rest. Bobby's now back playing at the Carlyle, but he sounds kind of *thumpy.* This, of course, is all hearsay because I couldn't get near the piano, or Dr. Ramsey, until way past eleven P.M.

Dr. Ramsey looked more ravishing than she ever had before. She was wearing something made out of long black velvet, with the front cut down below her navel, and a slit up her left leg to just under her left breast. With each forward movement she took it looked like she was stepping right out from under the whole thing, but it never happened. It was a night of unanswered prayer for every over, under, and in-between-sexed maleperson at the party.

Congressman Harry L. Hammond, who was being called "Mr. Vice-President" by everyone present, had finally caught up to Dr. Ramsey, and she was glad because even though *his* intentions were not *hers,* he offered some protection from the hordes of prowling, hot-pantsed Brazilians. She clung to Congressman Hammond's arm, which gave her every startling indication of getting longer and longer as she was tugged further into the pride of local lions. I expected it to snap back with a loud thunk or come off entirely and leave him there trying to figure a way to flick his Bic and hold his martini at the same time.

Hurd Cambridge was the front runner in this scrimmage, through sheer elbow power. Elizabeth Cambridge was never too far away from her super-charged spouse and watched him through the slitted eyes of a mother lynx. I had never seen her jealous before and I wondered why? Maybe before the arrival of Miss Lusty Tits, she figured that Hurd was just clowning, but Veronica Ramsey was more than a dusky native belle, more than a Wham-Bam-Thank-you-Ma'am-your-Hershey-bar-is-in-the-mail type. Veronica Ramsey was the kind of woman a man might take off with, the kind of a woman that Hurd Cambridge might take off with, which would leave Elizabeth with four million acres of Brazil nuts and a "Dear John" letter written in Portuguese.

A little later in the party I saw Elizabeth Cambridge and Mogo, the chief of the Pygmies, having a very heart-to-heart conference deep in the shady side of a giant potted palm. Elizabeth gave Mogo something that looked like money and he scooted away and left Elizabeth sitting there smoking a little black cigarillo and smiling. She blew a smoke ring that looked like that famous line drawing of Hitchcock.

31

"Ready for the excitement?" Cousin Shapiro whispered to me. It was just midnight.

"You mean, everybody is going to unmask?" I said.

"Nobody's wearing a mask," he said. I couldn't believe it.

"Mrs. Tooze isn't wearing a mask?"

"No."

"She looks like Peter Ustinov."

"Today she forgot to shave," Cousin Shapiro said. Then he moved in really close. I thought he was going to blow in my ear, "I asked you—are you ready for the excitement?"

"What excitement?" I said, not really caring. I was getting tired. I had had a long day counting rubber trees. The government had suddenly wanted to know, and counting rubber trees cannot only be the most tiring task in the world—it also is the most confusing. If your mind wanders for just one moment you have to start all over again. The trees seem to move as you're trying to line them up.

"I think the Angolans, the Nazis, the Israelis, the Chinese and maybe Pete El Jaguar are going to do something nutty—and maybe dangerous, too."

"I think I'll go home," I said. "Where's Reiko?" I started shoving through the crowd to find her. This was an impossibility. No one moved an inch. I thought I heard a scream—a wild female scream. I seemed to be the only one who had heard it. Or cared to have heard it. No one paid the slightest attention, although the scream was repeated—several times and with greater intensity and urgency.

I couldn't stand it and started opening doors in the direction of all this commotion. The screams were not of ecstasy. The third door was the one to the Cambridges' bedroom, now the Presidential Suite. I flung it open and immediately slammed it shut behind me because I had come upon a moving tableau the like of which I had never seen before: Veronica Ramsey, stark naked, running round and round the Presidential Suite, leaping over a double-king-size bed, closely followed by Mogo, the Chief of the Pygmies, and two of his fellows, all three of them naked and for Pygmies they all looked about one-third penis. Pancho Bocachica, the police chief, still handcuffed to the bedpost, was saying over and over, "Very nice. Very nice."

The action promptly stopped when I entered the room. Mogo made motions in sign language for me to take off my clothes and join in the fun. I shook my head, reluctantly(?), Veronica screamed and the chase was on again. Then *I* screamed something in Portuguese which was supposed to mean "Now Cut This Out!" but I think I said, "Where is the gentlemen's lounge?" I said it with so much authority, however, it scared the hell out of them and they weren't carrying their blowguns. This changed their minds about what they had in mind, whereupon they ran out through the French doors and disappeared into the undergrowth like three black baboons.

Veronica Ramsey, seemingly totally unaware of her nudity, came toward me, at which moment the door opened and Hurd Cambridge walked in. His mouth dropped a foot. "What the hell?" Then he turned and quickly locked the door. I threw somebody's dressing gown to Dr. Ramsey. "Douglas," Hurd said. "I think you've got some explaining to do."

"No, no," I said. "You first. Why did you invite Mogo the Pygmy to your party?"

"Mogo! He was here?"

"Yeah, and he brought two Pygmy Hell's Angel friends."

"What the hell are you talking about?" Hurd demanded. "Did you tear Dr. Ramsey's clothes off her?" He was awful loud now.

"I didn't *have* to!" I said, and I was louder than he was.

The French doors opened and the Reverend Meech, Cousin Shapiro, Mahareshi Nepal, the guru, and Pete El Jaguar slipped into the room.

"What is this?" Hurd was almost frothing now. "A gang-bang?" Then swinging around to Dr. Ramsey. "What, are they lined up outside, waiting their turn?" He was livid.

"Hurd," Dr. Ramsey tried to calm him, "you just don't—"

"Why didn't you tell me?" He was on the edge of the deep end. "I would have gotten my sleeping bag and slept outside your door, so I could've been first in line like they do at Yankee stadium. Jesus Christ! I've been the perfect stupid little gentleman for weeks, when everybody in town is—what's the fee? Fifty? A hundred? Two hundred?" he whipped out an enlarged roll of heavy bills. "Whatever it is—I'll pay it. I don't want the whole town pointing their fingers and going around saying, *"There he is.* The *only one* who didn't get a *piece* of the *action!"* Dr. Ramsey just stood there, tears coursing down her lovely face. She couldn't believe what she was hearing.

"Hurd!" There was something in my voice that stopped him. I used my Chicago tone, the one I used to use way back in the Capone days when I was a boy, helping out Uncle Al, convincing reluctant candy store owners a few slot machines couldn't hurt.

"Well," Hurd said, after a moment, "wouldn't *you* be sore if you found out that Reiko—"

The bedroom door knob turned. Then it started to rattle.

"There's somebody at the—" the Reverend Meech ventured.

"Let 'em wait!" Hurd said.

"You won't let anybody explain," I said. "Hurd, listen. I heard screaming and I opened the door and Mogo—"

"Where's Representative Hammond?" Cousin Shapiro said. "That's what we're here for—to protect him. I think somebody's gonna grab him for ransom."

"What?" Hurd said. "Who the hell would pay it?"

"That's a good question," Mahareshi Nepal said. "But *we* all came through the garden and the French doors—rather than call attention the other way—and—where *is* Representative Hammond?"

The bedroom doorknob rattled again this time much harder and a lot more insistent.

"It might be the police!" The Reverend Meech stage-whispered.

Pancho Bocachica, the police chief, still handcuffed to the bed-post, said, "Very nice. Very nice."

"Everybody!" the Reverend Meech yelled. "Under the bed! Quickly!"

The Reverend Meech was taking over and we all dove for under the bed, but under the bed was solid. There was no refuge there.

"*In* the bed! *In* the bed!" The Reverend was in full command now and we all jumped into the huge Hollywood bed. Hurd, Cousin Shapiro, Mahareshi Nepal, Pete El Jaguar, the Reverend Meech and me. Veronica had lost her robe and was right in the middle beneath the royal purple and gold of the Presidential Suite bedspread.

A key turned in the bedroom door and we all *sub-* and *uncon*sciously ducked under the covers. We stayed there motionless until we heard a loud gunshot. As one we all poked our heads out from under the royal purple and gold. It was Eizabeth Cambridge, standing in the middle of the bedroom right in front of the bed, smoking a long Egyptian cigarette and twirling a cute, but mean looking Baretta .38 caliber revolver.

Veronica's bare breasts had emerged (I guess she couldn't help it) over the top of the royal purple and gold, while the rest of us kept as covered up as we could.

Elizabeth was cool, I'll say that for her. She said to Veronica Ramsey, after looking over the rest of our popped up heads, "Only six at a time, my dear? I would have guessed you could have taken on an even dozen without even raising a sweat."

"Dear," Hurd said, after a long moment. "You've got this all wrong."

Elizabeth fired another shot from the Baretta into the gilded ceiling in reply to this.

The bedroom door opened again, and Representative Harry L. Hammond of Minnesota tiptoed into the room unaware for a slight moment of the drama being played there. Then suddenly, "OH. I didn't know anybody was here. This is my room." Then as he saw the group in bed, "Used to be my room."

"It's still your room," Elizabeth said, and fired another shot into the ceiling, this time bringing down a small chandelier.

"Harry," Veronica Ramsey called.

"Hmmmm?" Harry hmmmed, then slipped into his glasses. "Oh. Veronica—your bosom. And who are all these people?"

"Look," I said. "Mr. Hammond, you're in danger."

Elizabeth screamed with laughter at this.

Representative Hammond suddenly seemed to be more aware of the situation. "My dear," he said to Dr. Ramsey, indicating the six of us in bed with her. "Is this the reason for your requesting the United States government for an extra shipment of condoms?"

"Harry," Dr. Ramsey said. "I hardly know these people."

"But you're all in bed together!!!!" I felt that Harry Hammond's cool was leaving him, and I was beginning to feel as though I was part of a French farce, written by an inept French farce writer to be presented at some off-the-Boise playhouse—like in Minsk, Poland, or North Scranton, South Dakota. It was not only un-real, it was unbelievable and I'd had enough.

"I'm leaving," I said, throwing the royal purple and gold bed spread off me and getting to my feet.

Elizabeth put another shot into the ceiling, which was beginning to show signs of wear.

"I don't think so," she said.

"Give me that gun!" I said, as I had seen the brave TV police sergeants do a thousand times, and walked toward her. Another shot into the ceiling left me standing on one foot like a stork. Then there was a long pause. Things came to an abrupt standstill. I was getting a cramp in my upraised leg.

"Look, Elizabeth," I said. "I have to put my leg down." Elizabeth's reply was another shot into the ceiling. I thought, my god, their attic must be a mess by this time. I also wondered how many shots one could get out of a Baretta .38. Certainly no more than eight or nine. Elizabeth had to be running out, but prudently, I felt I shouldn't try to test my hypothesis. And thank the good lord, this was the moment that Mogo, the Pygmy chief chose to reappear. He was still naked, but this time his penis had modified from a mighty oak to a quaking aspen.

"Mogo," Elizabeth said, very calmly but with authority, "Go put some pants on—and don't *ever forget* you're a *Pygmy!*"

Mogo left.

32

A large group of tourists led by Lars Lindblad entered the Presidential Suite. "And this, of course . . ." Lars Lindblad seemed to be continuing something he had started outside the bedroom, "is, as I have told you, the Presidential Suite." Lars Lindblad apparently had done this tourist lecture so many times before that nothing could interrupt it. Either that, or he was nearsighted, because he completely ignored Elizabeth Cambridge standing there twirling her Baretta at the bare-bosomed Veronica in the huge Hollywood bed, surrounded by five men and me still holding up one leg that had long ago gone to sleep.

A small boy, who was mostly smeared chocolate, said matter of factly, "The lady *there's* got a gun, and the lady *there* in bed has her tits out."

"Yes," Mr. Lindblad continued. "Life on a nut plantation can be very interesting and did you know that in order to get nuts on a nut tree you must have a male nut tree and a female nut tree?"

"Which one has the nuts?" the small boy wanted to know, but he never found out, because at that moment Mr. Lindblad went right on talking and Elizabeth fired another shot through the ceiling while Mr. Lindblad kept talking and the large group of tourists kept listening and the little chocolatey boy started playing with his yo-yo.

The bedroom door opened in back of the large group of tourists, and Herr Braun and his platoon attempted to goosestep into the bedroom. It was a failure. Too many tourists were kicked and objected, and Mr. Lindblad put a stop to it. Braun's pseudo-Nazis were followed by six Angolans, who seemed bewildered, and by another group of Israeli soldiers, each carrying an automatic rifle and a loaf of Challah under their left arms. Then came three Chinese soldiers, some Russian army men, who seemed to be generals, and a few bearded bums, who were part of Castro's Elite Guard. The room immediately took on the atmosphere of the famous stateroom scene in that Marx Brothers' movie. It was crowded to the point of suffocation, but what panicked me was the fact that it was so jammed I couldn't get my leg down, and to add to the impossibility and implausibility of the scene was the sudden beating of the drums—the Angolans had brought tom-toms. I don't know whether they were signalling for help or they thought maybe someone would like to dance.

Herr Braun, the always efficient or maybe I should say seemingly efficient but more than likely just loud, shouted "Achtung! Achtung!" This word meant very little to the Angolans, the Cubans, the Russians, the Israelis, the Chinese, the Tourists, and Mr. Lindblad, who was continuing his lecture, oblivious. Mr. Lindblad was a very sincere man, who took his work seriously and no matter *what*, he was going to see to it that each and every tourist got what he had paid for.

Herr Braun switched to English. "Which one of you is Nelson Rockefeller?" Things got suddenly quiet. Mr. Brown repeated his question.

"Which one of you is Nelson Rockefeller?"

The room was as quiet as death. And it stayed that way.

Herr Braun waited as long as he thought decent then he said, "We have ways of making you talk!"

The whole thing was so ridiculous and I still couldn't believe that this wasn't some sort of a Barritos Passion Play, or whatever they called it, and everybody was just playing a part, and the whole thing was slowing down so the press notices couldn't help being anything but lousy. I blew.

"What the hell is going on!" I yelled at the top of my lungs. "Nelson Rockefeller is nine thousand miles away, asleep in his own little thirty-five-thousand-dollar bed! Let's cut out all this crap and continue the party out in the grand ballroom where it's supposed to be!"

"That lady there in bed has her tits out," the little boy repeated, and Elizabeth Cambridge fired a shot into the ceiling.

Everybody got out of bed and out of the room in a hurry. Everybody except Veronica Ramsey and the head man of the different ethnic army groups and Hurd, Elizabeth and me. Cousin Shapiro reentered the bedroom with the air of an old man who has just had a fantastically successful bowel movement.

"Well," Cousin Shapiro said, rubbing his Chinese hands together in anticipation of something. "How did everything go?"

"What," I said, "was supposed to go?"

"Everything," Cousin Shapiro said. "Mostly the kidnapping of Nelson Rockefeller." With this, the various military men surrounded Cousin Shapiro waving photos of Rockefeller.

"Yeah, yeah, yeah," Cousin Shapiro agreed. "That's Rockefeller all right. Yeah, you all got the right picture, but he ain't here. You've got Harry L. Hammond, the United States Representative from Minnesota. He's here—why don't you kidnap him. Maybe his family's got money, like maybe an old aunt who liked him when he was a boy."

This suggestion didn't arouse anyone.

"Wait a minute," Elizabeth Cambridge said. "That isn't the main issue here," and tried to fire a shot into the ceiling, but all she got was a dull click.

"Shit!" she said.

"Elizabeth," Hurd remonstrated. "*Ladies* don't fire shots into the ceiling of their bedrooms, and use vulgar language in front of distinguished guests."

"I'd like to fire one into her," Elizabeth said, indicating Dr. Ramsey who was back in a bathrobe.

"She didn't do a thing," I said.

"Oh, really," Elizabeth was at her bitchiest, now, "what was she doing in bed with six men—practicing for the Henley Regatta?"

"Hardly," Hurd said. "Bed is no place for rowing."

"It's a *water* bed, isn't it," Elizabeth said, almost triumphantly.

"Elizabeth," I said. "I saw the *whole thing*—"

"A study in black and white—like Whistler's mother."

"Mogo and his little men ripped my clothes off," Veronica said.

"Look!" she held up what was left of her beautiful black velvet. "I came in here to powder my nose and—"

"It's the truth," I said.

"If that's the goddamn truth," Elizabeth said, "What the hell were you all doing in bed with a naked broad when I came in?"

"That was Hurd's idea," I said like the goddamn big mouth I am.

"I'll *bet* it was," Elizabeth yelled and went for Hurd like a she-panther. After Cousin Shapiro had pulled her off Hurd and calmed her down and got her to believe the true story, Elizabeth reluctantly lent Veronica a gown and we all rejoined the party, where it seemed that *nobody* was mad at *nobody no more.*

The three Israeli soldiers who were supposed to take Mr. Brown back to Israel for trial as Wolfgang Bucholtz, the infamous Nazi art thief, were drinking and toasting each other like old friends. I couldn't help asking what the hell? The answer was simple. Mr. Brown's real name was Max Liebowitch. He was a nephew of one of the soldiers and he was from Tel Aviv where he had suffered a fire in his luggage shop; when he tried to collect the insurance the insurance company didn't believe it was an accident, and he had to get out of Israel in a hurry, so he fled to South America, since he didn't have any relatives in King's Point. He didn't have any relatives in Barritos either, but it seemed like a safe spot.

"Why," I wanted to know, and I thought it my duty to ask, or maybe I was just nosy. "Why were you drilling an army?"

"Have you ever been up against Allstate?" he asked.

One corner of the Cambridge Hacienda's Grand Ballroom was very quiet. Cousin Shapiro and the three Chinese soldiers were drinking Chinese tea and opening fortune cookies. I joined them for a moment, and learned that the three Chinese soldiers had decided not to go back to China. They said, in Chinese, to Cousin Shapiro, and Cousin Shapiro translated to me, they had had enough of Chairman Mao's goddamn endless period of mourning and they also wanted to wear sport clothes for once instead of those padded pajamas they had been forced into for so many years, and also the money they had brought over from China to pay the expense of kidnapping Nelson Rockefeller they were going to use to open up a chain of Western Auto Stores all over Brazil. They had it all figured out—they were going to undercut Sears and make a fortune.

The Cubans, and the Angolans, and the Russians were at loggerheads. They didn't know whether to go back to their native lands and admit failure and risk the firing squad or to stay in Brazil and cut rubber or pick nuts. I couldn't see where it was much of a decision. The Angolans, who could speak Portuguese, having lived for so long in Africa under the rule of Portugal, would have the easiest time adapting. The Cubans, who spoke only Spanish, which was somewhat close to Portuguese (in three or four words), felt they could pick up the language of Brazil in a few years, and they were awful goddamn tired of Castro's eight or nine-hour fireside chats which he delivered at the drop of a hat on Cuban TV, at which times, if you were caught not listening, they fixed it so you could never listen again.

The Russians were the most undecided of all. There were only six of them and they all had wives back in Russia, which helped them decide. They stayed.

Driving back home to our Casa Las Bombas, again we hit the giant anaconda who was hanging down our the road, this time with a different result. Luckily we got out of the car before the anaconda wrapped its coils around it—tighter and tighter.

Reiko and I walked home, and the next day we heard a rumor that an anaconda had swallowed a Volkswagen—with the engine running.

A month or so later when Marlin Perkins captured the anaconda for the St. Louis Zoo, it took fourteen gallons of Haley's M-O, but it finally worked, but from that day on the snake never ever sat down again.

I read all about it in Ranger Rick.

33

"Well, Veronica, your experiment doesn't seem to be going quite the way you expected it to, is it?" This was Harry L. Hammond, the representative from Minnesota, holding forth in our living room at Casa Las Bombas. Veronica didn't answer. She seemed to be making herself as small as possible on our enormous couch.

"I think she's done very well in such a short time," Reiko said, in a sort of women's lib protestive voice. "After all these people here are mostly ignorant savages."

"Yeah," agreed Bobby, who more and more was joining adult conversations. "They think babies are brought by the stork."

"I was found under a cabbage," Timothy said.

"That's why you didn't get wet," I said. "The cabbage kept the rain off you."

"Oh, come on, Papa," Timothy said. "I came out of Mommy's stomach, and so did Bobby."

"I came out first," Bobby said.

"You were always pushy," I said. Bobby laughed, but no one else did.

"I don't understand it," Dr. Ramsey said. "Why can't *these* people understand where a condom should be worn? They wear them anywhere *but*—on their *heads*, their *feet*, their noses, their *hands*—they blow them up and use them for kids' balloons."

"They don't have many toys," I said.

"No," Veronica snapped, "but they sure got plenty of kids! When the hell are they going to realize that they can't keep having them like a bunch of overheated rabbits!"

"The trouble is," I said, "from observation—I don't mean spying—is that they 'make love' upon the spur of the moment. They could be out gathering nuts, or tapping a rubber tree, and some damsel stops and bends over to adjust her sandals and wham-bam, José, or Mario, or Claudio, or Mogo or whomever, is into her like Roto-Rooter. They don't stop to slip a Ramses or a Trojan, there's no time. Dolores might straighten up and snap, the opportunity is gone forever."

"Who's Dolores?" Harry L. Hammond wanted to know.

"Doesn't have to be Dolores," I said. "It could be Maria, or Teresa, or Margie, or Linda, or Lucy-Ann."

"Or Charlie," Bobby said.

"Bobby!" Reiko said. "You're not supposed to be listening."

"How am I gonna learn," Bobby said. "From the Spiegel catalogue?"

"There must be a way," Harry Hammond insisted, "to make these people understand they must be—less careless."

"I've tried everything I could think of. I've spoken to them, through interpreters of course," Veronica said, "in Portuguese, Amerindian, Spanish, Greek, Mato Grosso, and Esperanto."

"How about English?" Timothy suggested. Timothy was learning rapidly to be a badass from his older brother.

Veronica shrugged her shoulders in resignation.

"Oh, come on now," Reiko said. "You're not going to give up, are you? The people down here love you."

"Then why," Veronica wanted to know, "why won't they wear my beautiful colored condoms? When they're making love they'll never even know they have them on. My God! Some of them put 'em on *afterwards!*"

"That's a step in the right direction," Harry L. Hammond said. "At least they know *what* to put them on."

"That's just *it!*" Veronica moaned. "They *don't!* They try to slip them over their testicles! It's *impossible!*"

"You know why?" Bobby said. What is this? I thought, what does *he* know?

"Why?" Veronica asked.

"Because the Witch Doctor, Doctor Momomoomoo, told them they were—" Bobby shot a sidewise glance at me, and then, "magic ball covers."

"What the hell!" I said. "What are magic ball covers supposed to do?" I found myself yelling a little.

"Cover your magic balls! What else?" Bobby yelled back.

"Anyone like-a tea?" Reiko asked, using her time-honored and worn ploy of trying to change the subject to something a little more G-rated. She also used this device to stop yelling and fights.

Hurd and Elizabeth Cambridge arrived and nobody wanted tea, but we did want a drink. I clapped my hands twice to summon Dolores, the maid. Dolores did not respond with alacrity. Dolores did not respond at all. I clapped my hands again—and again—and again. I felt like I was leading a Holy Roller meeting, and we were about to sacrifice a goat. I knew I was ready to sacrifice Dolores.

When Dolores finally shuffled in, the first thing Harry L. Hammond asked her was, "Dolores, do you bend over much to adjust your sandals?" As Dolores was about six months gone the only answer to this was "once."

After Dolores had wearily made her way to and from the bar and back to us with some very well made (like dynamite) Planter's Punches, and Pepsis for Bobby and Timothy, somehow we got back to the same subject, and after two more Planter's Punches each, the talk got pretty wild, and very interesting. We had long given up on Dolores tending bar and were taking turns (more or less) making our own drinks, which were now (more or less) pure alcohol (with just a pinch of vermouth, which has nothing to do with the making of a Planter's Punch, but it seemed like a good idea at the time).

Darkness was descending outside, as it always did about this time of night, and Claudio, our foreman, came in to give me the day's report on how many tons or pounds or gallons (or whatever) of latex had been gathered that day. I can't say that any of us were too interested and Claudio soon gave up trying to make sense to a bunch of weirdos who were making jokes about shrinking heads, humping, and other delicate subjects not intended for the tender young ears, which is of course why Bobby and Timothy were avidly listening.

We just couldn't let Claudio get away without a few drinks so he stayed, and contributed a very good thought. Claudio told us that the reason the poor and the ignorant people of Barritos were not using the condoms was because everything they ever got or bought from the United States came with instructions.

"My God!" Harry L. Hammond said. "It's so simple!"

"Yes," Claudio agreed. "But here, it's not. For instance, from the United States comes a pair of Levi's. The people here know how to put them on, but for years they never zipped up their flies, because there were no instructions!"

"Maybe that's the cause of the overpopulation problem. They don't know how to zip up!" Reiko said.

"They know now," Claudio said. "From Seventh Avenue, the Ladies International Garment Workers Union sent ladies down to show them, and as a side issue they picked up a few members here and there."

"Well, that's the goddamnedest thing I've ever heard," Veronica Ramsey said, kicking off her shoes and putting her beautiful little feet up on a coffee table.

"Yes," Harry L. Hammond agreed. "Today you got two choices if you want to work—the Teamsters or the Ladies Garment Union."

"Oh, Harry," Veronica said, impatiently, "That's not what I'm talking about! I'm talking about condoms. They need *instructions!* It sounds crazy! That's like needing instructions on *how* to *sit* on a *toilet seat!*"

Harry L. Hammond, trying to make his rather snubby nose more patrician, looked down it at Veronica and said with Kennedyesque disdain, "You've just brought up a point, my dear. Has it ever occurred to you that there may be people on this earth who *do* need instructions on how to sit on a toilet seat?"

"My father does," Reiko said. "That why he's so bowlegged."

"What?" I said.

"My father went to an American school in Tokyo, after the war, and for three years he used an American toilet."

"And that's why he's so bowlegged?"

"Yes, how did *he* know? For three years he sat—facing the wall."

Reiko and Bobby and Timothy and I and Dr. Ramsey all laughed, but Harry L. Hammond seemed a little stunned, "My God," he said, "Maybe *that's* why I'm bowlegged!"

34

"The way I see it," Hurd Cambridge said, "there seems to be only one solution to this condom problem, if they don't come with instructions."

There was a prolonged silence, and then Veronica Ramsey said, in a very small voice, "What's that?"

"A demonstration."

"A demonstration!" It was a Greek chorus.

"By whom?" Veronica said.

"*You're* the doctor," Hurd said.

"What do I do?" Veronica wanted to know. "Go from door to door with my little suitcase full of contraceptives, and yell 'Avon calling. Anybody with an erection in there?' "

"No, no," Hurd said. "That would take too long."

"Yes," Elizabeth agreed. "The simplest thing is a public demonstration."

"I've tried having meetings at the PTA, the DAR, the Rotary Club, the Elks. I've tried every organization I know of but nobody comes. How am I going to attract everyone in Barritos, at one time, and get it over with?" Veronica's was the voice of despair. "I even tried Alcoholics Anonymous!"

"What happened?" I asked. "Anybody show up?"

"All of them," Veronica said. "And they got up one by one and took an oath that they would never never take a drink out of the little rubber shot glasses I was showing them."

Everybody laughed and Veronica started to cry.

"Wait a minute," Hurd said. "That's a pretty funny story but, well, I'll have to admit I am not in favor of Dr. Ramsey's project,

180

because I need as many new nut pickers as I can get, especially when I have a good crop year, but I also realize that we do have a world over-population problem, and our children's children are going to be in trouble—it's that *close.*'' Then he turned to Veronica, and held her hands, while Elizabeth stiffened noticeably. ''Veronica,'' Hurd said. ''You've got to forget you're a lady, and remember you're a doctor. You're going to have to give a demonstration— right in the middle of the town square. It's the only place we have that's large enough to accommodate a crowd. Then you are going to have to select some—er—well-endowed young man, and—''

''Hung,'' Elizabeth Cambridge said.

''What?'' Hurd said.

''Hung,'' Elizabeth repeated. ''Well hung.''

Hurd hesitated for a moment and studied his wife. ''Is that the way they talk at Radcliffe?''

''Radcliffe, Vassar, Wellesley, Sarah Lawrence—''

''Forget it,'' Hurd said, and turned back to Veronica. ''Do you understand, Veronica?'' he said. ''We can't let happen what happened when Mrs. Tooze demonstrated with the condoms and the broom handle. I still see those broom handles all over town. They never caught on what the hell those colored condoms were really for. They just think they're pretty.''

''Hold it,'' Elizabeth said. ''You want Dr. Ramsey here to actually roll a condom on to some young man's stiff—''

''How else are you going to educate these innocent bastards!'' Hurd was shouting now.

''C'' Day or The Day of the Condom dawned bright and early because it was spring. It had been decided by us, our Planter's Punches and whatever else we had drunk the night before that Dr. Veronica Ramsey, the United States representative of contraceptives for all of Brazil, was duty bound to give the demonstration because she had sworn on the Bible back on the banks of the Potomac to carry out the work of the State Department and the United States Rubber Company.

A large platform, constructed in the middle of the town square, which looked like a boxing ring, further confused the natives. Rumors were flying that Muhammad Ali was due in to fight seven Pygmies with poison blowguns, and that the city of Barritos was going to pay Ali fourteen million dollars—win, lose or draw.

This wild underground report, abruptly changed around noon when the news broke that "Princess Grace and Mr. Grimaldi were dropping by to pick up some fresh Brazil nuts and watch a native dance or two and get the hell out." This bush telegraph scuttlebutt then became the well-substantiated (by no one) tale of Richard and Liz getting back together again. Word had it they were going to be remarried at the Barritos City Hall in a ceremony presided over by Dr. Momomoomoo and witnessed by three llamas, Lenny Bruce and a Nubian goat.

After the platform and the new grandstand (for dignitaries?) had been set up, the good citizens of Barritos learned the truth—there was going to be a big SEX SHOW!

By two-thirty P.M. there was standing room only in the town square, and they were standing on each other. The jungle telegraph was in full swing and some real savages, who were still nervous about eclipses and the volcano gods and who had never been out of the deep tangled mass of roots, vines, bamboo groves and leech-infested bushes of the Brazilian jungle, slunk into town singly or in small groups, their heads covered with toucan feathers and their faces tattooed and painted in grotesqueries not to be believed. Except by toucans.

Those who could, forced their way past these wild people of the deep shadows, past the curious locals and another boatload of Lindblad tourists, and into the Yacht Club where they proceeded to while away the afternoon in the best possible way.

Cousin Shapiro closed his Army and Navy store, placed the plywood riot boards over his plate-glass windows and went down to the square to help the Brazil Broadcasting Company set up their cameras.

"I don't know whether you should broadcast this 'live,'" Cousin Shapiro said to one of the Wide World of Brazilian Sports directors.

"Why?" the director said. "What are they gonna do in front of that crowd that we can't show to the rest of the country? Besides, the people are gettin' goddamn sick and tired of re-runs of Sonny and Cher's 'Whose Baby Is It *Really????*' "

Eight o'clock came and went. We were all underneath the ring platform in a makeshift dressing room. Reiko, me, Hurd and Elizabeth Cambridge, Cousin Shapiro, the Reverend Meech and his wife, and some other people I didn't know. Doctor Veronica Ramsey was also there, and being restrained by anybody who had the strength. She was screaming. Luckily the crowd outside—and there must have been thousands—were also screaming so they weren't aware of her violent protests, "I won't do it! I won't do it! I *can't* do it!"

"Think of the honor," I said, feeling like a fool.

"Honor!" Veronica shrieked. "Rolling a condom over a stiff prick is an honor?" I had never heard Veronica use such gutter language before, but I attributed it to stress.

"How am I gonna get somebody to demonstrate on, anyway? Anybody think of that?"

"That's easy," Hurd said. "You just call for volunteers."

"Volunteers! You mean there's gonna be more than *one?*"

"No," I said. "But it's like a magic show, you know. The magician calls for volunteers to be sawed in half."

"I wish somebody would saw me in half—and right now," Veronica moaned and moaned.

"That would make it tough on the rest of us," I said.

"What?" Veronica said.

"Trying to decide which half was best," I said.

"Jesus," Veronica said, "I'm about to be burned at the stake and you're telling jokes."

"I think you're making too much out of this, Veronica," Hurd said.

"Oh, yeah," Veronica said, her tone very Brooklyn now. "Suppose I call for volunteers and some faggot comes up there and I got to slip the condom over him and he's limp. There *can* be a *faggot Indian,* you know."

"No faggot is gonna volunteer!"

"You want a sure-fire volunteer. How about me," the Reverend Meech suggested, not too modestly.

"Of course," his wife, Norma-Lee agreed. "You'd be ideal. They're very religious, those savages."

"Only trouble is," Hurd said, "the good Reverend here has pronged every female for miles around. Maybe the husbands wouldn't accept the idea of . . ."

"Look," the Reverend Meech said, defending himself, "it's not my fault. It's the communion. These heathens don't believe in the wine and the wafer—so I had to give them *something!*"

"It's time!" The mayor of Barritos stuck his head into the makeshift dressing room.

Dr. Veronica Ramsey was dragged, fighting, and biting, and screaming, to the center of the ring platform. The surrounding thousands of natives, Indians, whites, blacks, browns, yellows, etc. were all doing the same thing. This, they felt, was going to be much better than a bull fight.

On the platform was a microphone and a waterbed. Veronica stood in front of the microphone looking long and hard at the waterbed. Then she turned to the microphone and then back to the waterbed again. Then she screamed and leaped off the ring platform right into the arms of Mogo, the Pygmy chieftain. He started up the aisle, but was quickly grabbed by everybody. Mogo thought it was a raffle and he had won something.

Back on the ring platform, Veronica stood at the microphone, seeming a lot more calm, with a look of determination that I felt would carry her through. An interpreter stood at her side. He had been sent up from São Paulo, and could speak all languages and all dialects indigenous to Brazil—north, south, east and west.

Veronica said (to the interpreter) "What's the waterbed for?"

The interpreter repeated to the crowd in three languages, "What's the waterbed for?"

The crowd hooted and screamed, shrieked itself into a frenzy of mirth. Undoubtedly this was the funniest thing that had *ever* been said in *Brazil*. There was more knee slapping in five minutes than on all of *Hee-Haw* for the past five years.

When things had more or less settled down into just a plain riot, Veronica asked for volunteers to model a new style of undergarment. This request took at least twenty minutes while the interpreter translated the request into Portuguese, Spanish, Amerindian, Greek, Japanese, Mato Grasso, Peruvian and Laplander.

There were no volunteers. Veronica looked over at all of us standing at ringside as if to say I told you so. She said to the interpreter, whom she was getting fed up with anyway, "Tell them all I need is one stiff cock—any size."

The interpreter translated this into seven languages and with each change of language the crowd grew more restless, as there was a great plethora of penises—stiff or otherwise.

"What do I do now?" Veronica yelled to us.

"Why don't you take your clothes off!" Hurd loudly suggested.

"Why don't you take a flying fuck for yourself!" Veronica gave him right back.

"Take your clothes off and I'll give it a try," Hurd said.

"This," Cousin Shapiro said, "is becoming vulgar."

"You got a mind like a steel trap, Shapiro," Hurd said. "Right away you can tell which way the wind is blowing."

"Watch it, you Limey bastard," Cousin Shapiro said. "We chased you out of Israel, we might do the same thing right here in Brazil."

"Wait a minute," I said. "Later we can all go up to the United Nations and have a talk with the Nathan's hot dog man. He's taking Kissinger's place for the summer." I explained. I was nervously doing Henny Youngman jokes—to cover up.

Veronica Ramsey was screaming into the microphone for volunteers for a condom fitting, but the huge mass was one large Babel. They didn't know what she was talking bout. The interpreter gave it another try in all the languages he knew and a few he made up. Somehow, it was either the way he said it or what he said, but he got to them, and Mogo, the Pygmy chief, along with the Watusi whom we had last seen as the humorous butler at the big Cambridge Festival party marched up the aisle. Mogo was like Napoleon and the Watusi like a barnyard Josephine—he wanted to go but he didn't want to go, but he went.

They were both boosted up onto the ring platform.

"Okay," shouted Veronica. "Drop your drawers."

The interpreter interpreted and both Mogo and the Watusi dropped what they had on—which wasn't much.

"Okay," Veronica said to the interpreter, "tell them what we expect!" While the interpreter translated this into Pygmy talk and Watusi, Veronica shouted over to us, "This is the most embarrassing moment of my life! I'll never be able to look a Watusi in the face again!" She then opened up a little purple box and took out two rolled condoms. She looked over at the two volunteers. Nothing, but absolutely nothing was happening. They were both as limp as licorice whips on a hot day.

Veronica took the interpreter aside and had a few words, then the interpreter had a few words with Mogo and the Watusi, and he told Veronica, "They say they wanna try it with you back in the bushes."

Veronica was off the platform in a flash, and Hurd, who was in pretty good shape, caught her and dragged her back to the platform. At the same time Cousin Shapiro shoved a large bunch of bananas at her.

"Here," Cousin Shapiro said, "use these for the demonstration!"

Veronica gave him a grateful smile, and felt that this might be the way out of this terribly embarrassing situation—bananas never went limp.

A table was hoisted up into the ring-platform and Dr. Ramsey proceeded to slip condom after multicolored condom over the stiff green bananas and roll them down tight. Soon all the bananas were encased in tight fitting rubbers, and when Dr. Ramsey held them up for everybody to see there was a lot of hissing and booing and cat-calling. This was the lousiest sex educational show they had ever seen!

Everyone scrambled for home, including us, which left the ring-platform empty except for Mogo and the Watusi, who stood in the center of the ring acknowledging the absolute non-attention they were getting. They were shaking hands with themselves like they had both just won the world's championship, and both sported erections which they could have used to karate-chop their way through six building-blocks had they the mind to.

"You had your chance!" Veronica yelled back over her shoulder.

This demonstration, which happened almost three years ago now, had a great effect on Brazil's economic position the world of agriculture. They used the condoms exactly as Veronica had shown them. It has taken the farmers this long to discover that condoms kill bananas, and United Fruit went bankrupt without ever knowing why.

Read on.

NEW YORK—As evidence that condoms are, at last, becoming more popular around the world, *Forbes* magazine reports that in Brazil, some cities have begun accepting them as tokens on public buses.